Be Water, My Friend

Be Water,
My Friend

The Teachings of
BRUCE LEE

Shannon Lee

FLATIRON
BOOKS
NEW YORK

www.flatironbooks.com

All photographs courtesy of the Bruce Lee Family Archive

Dragon illustration based on © Nipatsara Bureepia/ Shutterstock.com

Designed by Donna Sinisgalli Noetzel

Library of Congress Cataloging-in-Publication Data

Names: Lee, Shannon, 1969– author.
Title: Be water, my friend : the teachings of Bruce Lee / Shannon Lee.
Description: First U.S. edition | New York : Flatiron Books, [2020]
Identifiers: LCCN 2020031675 | ISBN 9781250206688 (hardcover) | ISBN 9781250794833 (international, sold outside the U.S., subject to rights availability) | ISBN 9781250206695 (ebook)
Subjects: LCSH: Martial arts—Philosophy. | Spiritual life. | Lee, Bruce, 1940–1973.
Classification: LCC GV1101 .L44 2020 | DDC 796.8—dc23
LC record available at https://lccn.loc.gov/2020031675

Our books may be purchased in bulk for promotional, educational, or business use. Please contact your local bookseller or the Macmillan Corporate and Premium Sales Department at 1-800-221-7945, extension 5442, or by email at MacmillanSpecialMarkets@macmillan.com.

First U.S. Edition: 2020
First International Edition: 2020

10 9 8 7 6 5 4 3 2 1

To my father.

For my daughter.

For you.

Contents

Introduction		3
1. The Water Way		11
2. The Empty Cup		33
3. The Eternal Student		56
4. The Opponent		81
5. The Tools		104
6. The Obstacle		132
7. The Rainstorm		150
8. The Living Void		166
9. The Way of the Intercepting Fist		188
10. My Friend		208
Epilogue		225
Acknowledgments		227

Be Water, My Friend

Empty your mind.

Be formless, shapeless, like water.

You put water into a cup; it becomes the cup.

You put water into a teapot; it becomes the teapot.

You put it into a bottle; it becomes the bottle.

Now water can flow, or it can crash!

Be water, my friend.

Introduction

When I was growing up, my mom used to tell my brother and me not to tell people that Bruce Lee was our dad. She said, "Let people get to know you for who you are without that information." It was great advice, and for many years I skirted the issue in every conversation I could. Of course, my friends would always find out eventually when they'd come over and see our family pictures on the walls. However, with most elementary school–age girls, that just meant a curious shrug of the shoulders before we put on our roller skates or rode our bikes. But as I became an adult, I began to feel like I had a secret I was guarding, and the conversations became more difficult to avoid, especially after I started looking after my father's legacy full-time. If I skirted all the typical icebreaker questions such as "So what do you do?" and "And how did you get into that?" I started to feel not only like I was hiding, but actually lying through misdirection, and it didn't feel good. After all, I'm not ashamed to be Bruce Lee's daughter—I'm honored.

I would say, though, that being Bruce Lee's daughter and having people react to that piece of information in such overwhelming ways has made it a challenge to my own identity at times. Perhaps that's why I feel like my father's core philosophy of self-actualization (yes, Bruce Lee was a philosopher!) resonates so deeply with me. How does one honor the plain fact of their DNA while at the same time understanding that it doesn't mean anything about one's own soul? Or does it? Throw in my decision to spend a good portion of my life protecting and promoting the legacy of one of the humans who gifted me this life and who has meant so much to me, and questions of identity start to get pretty muddy.

"What do you remember about your father?"

It's the question I'm most frequently asked and one that used to deeply disturb me because I couldn't answer it with clarity. My father died when I was just four years old, so I don't have many of my own stories or dazzling pieces of wisdom he passed on to me directly the way his contemporaries do. I don't have a letter he had written to me specifically. And how could I explain that, despite this, I feel I know him so essentially? How could I articulate that I feel I understand him in a way that others who "knew" him might not even understand him?

I have come to recognize that these feelings—of what his essential nature is—are my memories of him. I know him in a way that's unclouded by any conflicts or hurts, jealousies or competition, or even any overly romanticized notions. I know his love, his energy signature. I know it because in our formative years, that is how we know our parents—through what we take in through our senses. Most children don't have fully formed, cognitively mature memory in play until much later than the age of four. We have to learn over time how to interpret and interact with what we are taking in per our cultural constructs. And that's why we so often get things wrong as children; we assign meaning incorrectly because we can't understand the subtleties of the whole of what is going on. We haven't had the life experience yet. But we do feel the essential quality of everything, in some ways more keenly than our adult counterparts. My father shined his loving light on me, and I remember that clearly. I remember his essential nature. I remember him.

My father was a truly phenomenal specimen of a human being in many ways—intelligent, creative, learned, skilled, driven. He worked really hard to cultivate every aspect of himself. At one point he said, "Some may not believe it, but I spent hours perfecting whatever I did." He worked not only at sculpting his body but at shaping his mind, educating himself, evolving his practices, developing his potential. He also worked at the little things, like having beautiful handwriting, writing and speaking grammatically well, developing a colloquial understanding of English through joke-telling, learning how to direct a film—the list goes on and on. And as a result, he created a legacy that continues to be relevant forty-seven years after his death.

But if there's one thing I've learned through the practice and understanding of his philosophy, it's that you don't need to be Bruce Lee in order to make the most out of your life. Trust me. As his daughter, the self-imposed stress to be one-tenth the specimen of a human that he was and in the *way* that he was has been overwhelming, paralyzing, and terrifying. It has stopped me in my tracks several times in my life.

But that's when I take a deep breath and remember: Bruce Lee doesn't want me to be Bruce Lee. Thank god. And what you'll discover in this book is that what Bruce Lee wants is for you to be the best version of *you* that you can be. And that will look entirely different from Bruce Lee because, well, you are you. And guess what. Bruce Lee himself was not good at a *lot* of things. He could barely change a light bulb or cook an egg. I'd like to see him try to put together some IKEA furniture. (In my imagination, it ends up smashed to splinters, with the Allen wrench sticking unceremoniously out of the drywall where it has been hurled in abject frustration.) But that aside, his words should encourage you to consider a process of self-actualization whereby you take a look at who you may actually and essentially be—where you notice what your potential is pulling you toward and how to work to cultivate *that*. What will emerge will be just as unique, just as bright, just as uplifting, and just as energized as my father was, but in your own way and in your own process. And not only that, but you will end up with a centered sense of purpose that will bring you much more peace of mind and joy.

That's why I got into this, after all. It wasn't the cool T-shirts (although the T-shirts are cool). It was because, as you will come to learn, I have been deeply moved and healed by these practices and words myself. I wouldn't have dedicated such a huge portion of my life to promoting my father's legacy if I didn't earnestly feel it was worthy of my time and promotion. I want you to get to know this deeply philosophical and inspirational side of my father as I know and experience him. I want you to get any little tidbit or morsel you can that contributes something of value and goodness to your life. And I hope you connect with my family's stories that are within these pages and find something of yourself in them.

So what qualifies me to be your guide? I should tell you up front that I'm not a researcher or an educator or a therapist or even a life coach. I have no expertise in anything other than Bruce Lee. And even that is a particular kind of expertise not based on a vast knowledge of dates and times and events. My expertise is in having known and been loved by him, in having gratitude for the gift of him, in living his words as best I can, and in trying diligently to find my own self.

And even without all the degrees and expertise, I've still written this book as part prescription, part allegory, part revelation. For those of you far along on your spiritual journey, this book may seem simplistic at times. It's meant to be. I'm hoping to provide access to these ideas to the biggest swath of people possible. But the further you get in the book, the deeper the messages will get. I hope you will stay with me to discover where the waterways flow.

In this book, I'll do my best to impart to you what my father's "Be Water" philosophy is and how I understand it from having been immersed in his life and legacy for many years now. For those of you who are unfamiliar with this quote of my father's, it first came into his understanding around the practice of martial arts, which we will use as a metaphor throughout this book for living one's most engaged life. But most important for me, the idea of being like water is to attempt to embody the qualities of fluidity and naturalness in one's life. Water can adjust its shape to any container, it can be soft or strong, it is simply and naturally always itself, and it finds a way to keep moving and flowing. Now imagine if you could learn to be that flexible, that sentient, that natural, and that unstoppable? For a martial artist like my father, this would be the height of technique. For me, it is the height of my ability as a human to be self-expressed, powerful, and free.

I truly believe, and I'm not the only one, that my father was actually one of the more notable and profound philosophers of the twentieth century. It's just that not many people know him in that way because he was an action film star and a martial artist—and thereby somehow easier to dismiss as an intellectual. When we think of a philosopher, we typically think of someone who is scholarly, published, or who may give inspirational and educational talks. We don't think of an action movie star. But my father was much more than that, as you will come to find out, through the way he lived his life and the words he left behind.

It might surprise you to find out that I'm not that precious about the material. I'm not a Bruce Lee purest about anything other than his *energy*. I do not practice an academic exactitude with his words. Where I have found it useful to illustrate what I want to say, I have combined quotes and edited quotes to make them more digestible. I use different types of language (slang, colloquialism, cultural reference) to get my point across in as utilitarian a way as possible. And I will tend to default most often to masculine gender pronouns because my father's words typically express that way, but please know that this book is meant for you—whoever you are, however you identify.

For the most part, I'll still just be skipping stones along the surface of the depth that exists within these thoughts and ideas. This book covers many concepts that whole books have been written about and whole practices developed around, and thus it's not a fully instructive deep dive into any one area. Rather, it's best to view this as an introduction to the prospect of a life of rich exploration and profound possibility. And, as your guide, you should know I'm still learning and growing too. But, as my father said, "The good life is a process, not a state of being. It is a direction, not a destination."

Before you dive in, I want to alert you to the naturally circuitous nature of this material. At one point I'm going to suggest to you that you need to apply your willpower, and several pages later I'm going to suggest that you yield your will. It is possible that you'll get frustrated by the seeming contradictions. But they aren't really contradictions. They are just different responses for ever-changing circumstances. Keep in mind that my father's philosophy, and more specifically the "Be Water" principle, is really an ecosystem that encompasses the entirety of existence. Try to hold on to the idea of the nature of water (its pliability, its aliveness) when that happens, and I'll do my best to be clear.

Most important, we're not aiming to adopt a rigid stance or program toward anything. This is a book about water, after all. And life is not rigid or programmed either. Just ask the sudden flat tire or the unexpected bonus. We need to make space and allow for all of life's twists and turns, ups and downs, while learning to be flexible, sentient, natural, and unstoppable in the midst of it all. Learning to maximize your potential and flow in your total being is not going to happen overnight, and the first time you get a taste of success and think that you've got it all figured out, you'll stumble in the face of some new challenge, all your old conditioning will raise its ugly head, and frustration will make you want to pound your fists against the wall. And in this moment you will get to make the choice, once again, to either shut down or grow.

In those instances, try to remember these words of my father: "People have to grow through skillful frustrations, otherwise they have no incentive to develop their own means and ways of coping with the world." And it's true. If you never attempt anything hard or challenging, the first time something hard or challenging happens to you, you will be knocked on your ass and not know what to do. Or you might want to curl up in a ball and cower on the floor. So try to look upon frustration as your teacher or, dare I say, your friend. Try to listen to what it has to say to you and about you, about your capacity, about your beliefs, about where you need to stretch a bit, about what you really want and love, and let it guide you to a full understanding of yourself. I promise you that over time your life will open up and you will start to feel more powerful and more free.

As we go on this water journey together, we'll also talk about energized focus and joy. We'll talk about how to handle defeat and changing circumstances. We'll talk about how to cultivate faith in oneself and faith in this process, how to be actively aware within your life, and how to be centered and achieve peace of mind.

It's exciting work, but it is work. There are going to be mistakes. There are going to be blocks. But we are playing the long game. We are in this practice for a lifetime. Life, after all, is meant to be fully lived. We want to approach it with a sense of full involvement and engagement. We want to look for the things that speak to us and foster our optimism as we practice this over the full term of a life. We can submit that it will require effort, that there will be failures, but hopefully we can accept that from these we can learn and grow and become ever better still. We will learn to adopt a proper stance toward our practice of becoming our best self that is both relaxed and ready. And, most important, let's remember that we are not trying to be Bruce Lee. We are trying to be wholly ourselves.

And, by the way, you've already begun. We've been practicing at this in fits and starts all our lives. We may not have been fully aware of it, but we've all been trying to make the best of our lives. Of course we have! The thing this book offers is just another point of view on how one might do that. By being intrigued enough to pick up this book and see how it might speak to you, you already know you are interested in taking another step down the path of considering something more for yourself. So let's attempt to flow with the stream, and let's make it fun. Let's make it a grand experiment.

After all, this is really supposed to be about finding what you love, what energizes you, what your dreams are, and who your most essential self really is. So get ready, and, in the words of my father, attempt to hold this perspective as we make our way forward:

> Do not be tense, but ready; not thinking, but not dreaming; not being set, but flexible. It is being wholly and quietly alive, aware, and alert; ready for whatever may come. . . .

I

The Water Way

Water may flow swiftly or it may flow slowly,
but its purpose is inexorable, its destiny sure.

Martial arts was my father's chosen love. From the age of thirteen, when he started practicing wing chun, until the end of his life at age thirty-two, he practiced every single day with little exception. He said of his passion for martial arts, "Everything I have learned, I have learned through the practice of martial arts." He had an extraordinarily sharp and insightful mind, and I often think it was a brilliant piece of fate that a mind like his was attached to such a physical and combative practice.

As it turns out, martial arts *is* a perfect metaphor for life. There are few disciplines where the stakes are so personal and so high as in a fight. Proficiency in martial arts is the practice of keeping centered and skillfully responsive under the direst of circumstances: the threat of physical harm. When you have mastery in combat, you not only meet a fight with composure and skill, you become an artist of movement, expressing yourself powerfully in the immediate, unfolding present with absolute freedom and certainty. When your personal safety or very life is on the line, to remain alert, mobile, and skillful is an immense feat of self-mastery.

This philosophy of movement was how Bruce Lee lived every aspect of his life. He was always after what I like to call "the real." Real fighting. Real living. Street-tested concepts. Everyday applications. He didn't deal in points earned or light touches landed, as was the style of the day in high-level competitions. He called that kind of point-oriented, competitive fighting, with so many rules on how to score without causing injury, "dryland swimming."

That's not to say he was going around challenging everyone to a street fight, though he did fight a handful of real challenge matches in his lifetime. What he did do was train all out. While protective gear did exist in a variety of arts, he was among the first to repurpose many separate pieces to create true sparring equipment for whole-body, full-contact engagement. He made focus mitts out of baseball gloves by flattening them and filling them with padding. He repurposed baseball catcher chest plates and boxing gear as well as kendo knuckle-finger gloves. This kind of sparring equipment has evolved and is commonplace now, but back in the 1960s, its use was unheard of in Chinese kung fu (or, as my father pronounced it in his native Cantonese, "gung fu").

Through heavy physical training and combat, my father had the opportunity to translate principles between mind and body—from idea to action—on a constant basis. Most (and possibly all) of what he espoused philosophically started first as an approach to being a successful martial artist. Then, as with all universal principles, he ultimately realized that these martial arts applications were broad and deep—and inimitably applicable to the art of being human.

But let's begin at the beginning.

A Boy, a Kung Fu Master, and a Boat

My father began studying wing chun gung fu in Hong Kong at the age of thirteen. His sifu (or teacher) was a man by the name of Yip Man (also Ip Man). Yip Man was a very skillful teacher who not only drilled physical techniques but also wove in Taoist philosophy and the principles of yin and yang into his lessons. He often illustrated his teachings through parables on nature, such as using the difference between an oak tree and bamboo to make a point (the oak tree will eventually snap under a strong wind while the bamboo survives because it can move with the wind).

My father was a dedicated student and a quick learner. He practiced outside of class whenever he could and became a star pupil. But he was also a teenager—a teenager whose childhood nickname had been Mou Si Ting, which translates to "Never Sits Still"—and whose later nickname and stage name was Siu Loong, or "Little Dragon." Born in the hour of the dragon and the year of the dragon, young Bruce Lee was all fire, all "yang." And Yip Man was forever trying to teach this fiery teen the importance of gentleness, fluidity, and pliability, not just strength and cunning.

To my father's credit, he would listen and try, but his eagerness (and his temper) would get the better of him; and besides, he'd wonder, isn't it better to win however you can? What does gentleness have to do with winning really?

One day, Yip Man was trying to teach young Bruce to relax and calm his mind, to forget about himself and follow his opponent's movements instead. Essentially, he was trying to get him to practice the art of detachment—to respond intuitively to an opponent rather than get caught up in only his own strategy, obsessively calculating his own punches and moves. When my father would get in his own way, visibly trapped in his own cleverness and combativeness, sweat dripping off his furrowed brow, Yip Man would step in again and again and tell him to conserve his energy by going with the natural bend of things. "Never assert yourself against nature," he told him. "Never be in frontal opposition to any problem, but control it by swinging with it." Finally he stopped young Bruce and said, "Don't practice this week. Go home and think about what I've said."

Don't practice this week?! That was like telling my father not to breathe for a week. Banished from class, Bruce did continue to practice on his own, and he meditated and struggled in solitary contemplation to understand what his teacher was trying to say. Frustrated, and with pent-up energy to spare, he decided one day to take a small boat out onto Hong Kong harbor with his newly found and highly resented free time.

He stopped rowing after a while and just lay in the boat, letting the waves take him. While he rocked along, he began to replay in his mind his teacher's urgings and all the time he had spent on training. What was he doing wrong? Why couldn't he understand what his teacher was saying? It didn't make any sense! His frustration spiked. In his fury, he leaned over and punched the South China Sea several times with all his might.

Suddenly a thought struck him, and he stopped and looked down at his wet hand. My father later wrote about it in this essay:

> Had not this water just now illustrated to me the principle of gung fu? I struck it but it did not suffer hurt. Again, I struck it with all my might—yet it was not wounded! I then tried to grasp a handful of it but this proved impossible. This water, the softest substance in the world, which could be contained in the smallest jar, only seemed weak. In reality, it could penetrate the

hardest substances in the world. That was it! I wanted
to be like the nature of water.

He had a second revelation as he watched a bird fly overhead and
cast its reflection on the water in the very next moment:

> Should not the thoughts and emotions I have when in
> front of an opponent pass like the reflection of the bird
> flying over the water? This is exactly what Professor Yip
> meant by being one in whom feeling was not sticky or
> blocked. Therefore in order to control myself, I must
> first accept myself by going with and not against my
> nature.

And thus began my father's long and intimate relationship with water,
an element that is soft yet strong, natural yet able to be directed, de-
tached yet powerful, and, above all, essential to life.

No Martial Arts Experience Necessary

At this point, you may be thinking, "I'm not a martial artist; how is
this book going to apply to me and why do I care about the epiphany
of a seventeen-year-old from more than sixty years ago?" Don't worry.
While we will be talking about martial arts from time to time, it will
only be by way of metaphor and for the illustration of concepts that
are applicable across general human experience. Sometimes I find it
easier to digest abstract ideas through a more grounded physical example. As to why we may care about being like water, my father's philosophical ideas, coupled with the way he lived his life, have inspired

people the world over, including myself, to transform our lives for the better. And the way he lived his life was by way of water's example.

At its essence, water flows. It finds its way around (or even through) obstacles. My father would call this having "no limitations." Water is present to its circumstances and surroundings and therefore ready to move in any direction that allows it passage. That openness and pliability means it is in a constant state of readiness, but a natural readiness because it is simply being wholly itself. To be like water, then, is to realize your most whole, natural, and actualized self where you are living as much as possible in the slipstream of life as you forge your own path forward.

Trust me when I say there is something in these pages for you whether you are an athlete, a stay-at-home mom, a student, a musician, an accountant, an entrepreneur, a cop, or whatever shape of human you take. Remember, though, that, at the same time, not everything in this book may be for you. You should never just take something hook, line, and sinker because someone else told you it was true. What is true for one may not be true for another—or the path to a shared truth may look very different for you than for someone else. There's no one piece of advice nor one set of tools that will fit everyone. I can't tell you what will work for you—only you will know what that is as you try some of these things on. I'll share my family's stories and my thoughts, experiences, and ideas. The rest is up to you. And if you don't find anything helpful here, don't give up. There are many resources in this world. Keep seeking, and you will find what you're looking for.

So let's metaphorically bow in, shall we? Every martial arts lesson starts with a bow. It's not a subservient thing. It's an intention thing. I'm here. I've shown up. I'm paying attention and I'm ready to participate.

Thank you for being here. Now let's start with some water basics.

No Limitation

Why is the idea of being like water such an important principle of my father's? After all, my father's core tenet that he coined to represent his art and his life was actually this:

Using no way as way, having no limitation as limitation.

But doesn't that describe the nature of water perfectly? For anyone who has ever had to contend with a leak, it is sometimes baffling how the water got in and ended up where it did. Sometimes you have to rip the whole wall or ceiling apart to find out where it's coming from and how it's traveling to its destination.

Just recently I had such an experience, with a terrible leak in my office. We were pretty sure it was coming through from the roof, but it wasn't just dripping down from a hole directly above. It was springing up in all kinds of places and seeping through the wall on the upper floor. The landlord sent someone to fix it three times, but without any obvious point of entry, the basic attempts the repairman made were not getting to the root of the problem. So we kept our tarps and buckets in place on the upper floor, thinking that everything on the floor below was relatively safe.

Then it rained again, and torrentially this time. And because the water had been getting into the wall on the upper floor, it just continued down its path through the wall, hit the ceiling beneath, and ran along the beams. When we returned the next day, water was dripping off the ceiling beams across the expanse of the first floor—it was literally raining indoors.

Distressing as it was for us, why is this admirable on the part of the water? Well, the water was not to be deterred. It was going to find a path, or even multiple paths. It would move along until it met with an obstacle, and then, if it needed to, it would change course and keep on flowing. It used "no way" as its way. In other words, it used every possible way. And it ran along without limitation. Even though we have since patched the roof, the rainwater is still undeterred in finding its way, though now it does so outside the building instead of inside. Thankfully.

This is the basic way of water. It is unstoppable. And though the word *water* is reflected nowhere in my father's core tenet above, the phrase represents perfectly one of the preeminent water basics that I want us to begin to sit with—that water is undeterred. It will carve canyons into mountains over centuries. And when I say I want us to "sit with" this, I use this term because I don't want us to only think about it. After all, life isn't only a mental exercise. When I say "sit with," I mean be with it—consider it, notice it, experience it, feel it, and allow it in.

Let's think of water as unstoppable, similar to how many people think of Bruce Lee as unstoppable. Whether you know anything about him or not, you likely still have a picture of a heroic, skilled badass who plowed through his opponents—whether in real life or just in the movies.

So what does it take to be unstoppable like water?

Be Aware

For my father, being "in the flow" meant, in part, being present—choosing to live his life consciously, purposefully, intentionally. Being present means more than occupying physical space. It's not just about whether you show up for class, but whether you are actively participating in class. Are you listening, asking questions, taking notes, engaging in the conversation? Or are you physically there but on your phone, half asleep, hoodie up, earbuds in? Being present is a key component of being like water. Why?

Well, if the rainwater from my example above were not in active participation with its environment at every moment, then it would not have found its way into my office. That is the nature of water. We, however, get to choose whether to stop at the first obstacle or keep going, unlike water, which *always* chooses to keep going if given the opportunity. And, remember, even seemingly still waters are fed by deep, rumbling springs or consistent rains and snowmelt, else they go fetid or ultimately evaporate. So if we want to fulfill our human potential, then we can't let ourselves be complacent or stopped either—we have to find our way forward and keep being replenished again and again. And in order to find our way, we need to be paying attention. We need to be aware of what is happening all around us.

My father has a quote that I love, which reads, "To grow, to discover, we need involvement, which is something I experience every day, sometimes good, sometimes frustrating." You might think, "Well, isn't everyone involved in their own lives?" The truth of the matter is that while, yes, we are involved in the sense that we are alive, as in breathing and doing things, many of us are not fully tapping into our consciousness, our self-awareness, and, ultimately, our potential. We are not proactively directing the course of our lives and paying attention to and working with our energy and the environments and relationships we find ourselves in. For many of us, life happens *to* us. We get trapped in unconscious patterns of living and forget that there are, in fact, many choices and many ways to be *fully involved* in the creation of our lives. To say it another way, we want to be fully alive versus merely subsisting. And to do that, we have to be paying attention.

That's not to say that we must always be "on," always in control, always "in the zone." That could be exhausting. And such a life may not be possible for most of us 24/7, because, as we know, life is not always within our control. Challenging things happen to us from out of the blue. We get fired. We get sick. We experience a sudden loss. Or we just get tired and tune out sometimes. But this notion of cultivating a Bruce Lee "water practice" is one of heightening our awareness and acquiring and sharpening our tools so that we have the capacity to encounter life, and whatever life throws at us, with as much skill, consciousness, and grace as possible—while finding our ultimate way.

And presence and awareness play a big part in that. If my mind is polluted with all manner of negativity or I'm snapping at people out of pure emotional reaction, then I am not responding—I am reacting. If I am not aware of how I am feeling or what thoughts are going through my head, then how do I change bad habits or find more happiness and personal satisfaction? I need to be able to observe myself in order to see what I need to amend. If I am paying attention, then I can see what's happening all around and within me, and only then am I free to choose how I want to participate. You can't choose a response if you can't even see that there are choices to be made.

Imagine for a moment what it would be like if you had the capacity and the skill to choose your response to every situation in every moment rather than being overtaken by impulsive reaction. What if you didn't get carried away by your emotions or shut down and become paralyzed in the face of some challenge? Imagine what it would feel like to be fully present to every experience without losing yourself in it. What it would feel like to have the perfect response that reflected exactly who you are in every situation without taking it on and being personally affronted by it. It would feel powerful, right? And I understand that as great as that imaginary, powerful life sounds, it may also feel unrealistic right now. That's okay. We are going to talk about this realistically and humanely as we go because we are not meant to be perfect. That's right: *we are not meant to be perfect.*

To be like water is not to be aspiring to perfection. Perfection is a difficult master. To be like water is not to be controlling of everything. Control is a tight yoke. For now, let's consider perfection and control like this.

There is perfection in the constant and imperfect unfolding of life, for every imperfection creates the opportunity for me to learn something that I can then grow from and put into practice. By practicing that which challenges me—practicing acceptance, practicing patience, practicing loving, practicing improvement—I will gain confidence until the skill I am practicing becomes second nature. Perfection as we typically think about it should be treated more as a way to focus our attention rather than a final accomplishment that we attain. To come to terms with this notion is to be able to view the imperfections of life as the perfect teaching tools and opportunities for our own growth and betterment, rather than a measure of our success.

And then there's control. In the astrology book *The Secret Language of Birthdays* by Gary Goldschneider and Joost Elffers, each day of the year has a name or title associated with it. I am born on "the Day of Solid Control." Good grief. I don't think most people I know would characterize me as the classic control freak (at least I hope not). I feel I've had enough things happen to me that were beyond my control that I am more apt to throw up my hands in surrender and make the most of a situation than to try to bend everything to my will. However, there's a balance to be struck here. And maybe it's in practicing how much control I can exercise through "not controlling." Where can I see the path opening up in the wake of a challenge? How much can I enact my will toward whatever goals I have, while at the same time making space for what is actually happening, in the midst of life's journey?

Recently I had a big project that I really believed in, and it did not go as planned. More than that, it seemed to be failing big-time. So I tried to control it by moving heaven and earth to get the right people in place and get the necessary changes to happen to keep things on track, all while we were running out of money and options fast. I loved the project. I wanted to keep it going, but the cards just weren't turning up in my favor. So I decided in the eleventh hour to stop resisting what was clearly happening. It was messy. I had investors with expectations. I had to lay people off and shut things down. But I decided to be present with what was happening and stop resisting it. I gave the future of the project to the universe, and I said, "Show me the way." And like water, I began to follow the course of this new unfolding rather than try to build a thousand dams to enforce the direction of the stream.

Yes, one phase of the project ended, but out of it came some new ideas (better ideas!) and new potential partners and possibilities. And the most important thing was that by letting go and following the natural way of things, I wasn't giving up or failing. I was finding a new way, and I reduced my stress and my anxiety while gaining more energy as well. And even though I still don't know if this project will be successful, I continue to be able to be present with it, to show up and give my energy where I need to give it and let the rest of it unfold naturally. The difference is that I'm no longer trying to control the destiny of this whole complicated venture, nor am I trying to perfect it. I'm participating and cocreating, but no longer forcing.

My father said, "Here is natural instinct, and here is control. You are to combine the two in harmony." And so I constantly try to ask myself how much "control" I can exercise within my perfectly imperfect self to be fully present and accountable in the face of challenging scenarios and people—such that I get to realize some new way of being for myself and all I create. Sometimes I'm not very successful, and there is bountiful learning in the reflection of what could have been done differently. But all the growth and learning, whether in the moment or later, only gets to happen if I am fully present to and aware of my internal and external experiences.

Be Pliable

> When man is living, he is soft and pliable; when he
> is dead, he becomes rigid. Pliability is life; rigidity is
> death, whether we are speaking of the body, the mind,
> or the spirit. Be pliable.

One of the simplest and most easily grasped lessons of water is its pliability. Throw a rock in a stream, the stream adapts to make space for the rock. This is one of the lessons my father received as a teenager that day he realized that water was a metaphor for gung fu. When he tried to grasp the water, it ran through his fingers. When he tried to punch the water, it moved out of the way of his fist and did not suffer harm. My father went on to speak often about the importance of gentleness and pliability when it comes to life and martial arts.

He also frequently recounted the lesson of the bamboo and the mighty oak tree in the storm as relayed to him by his sifu. The rigidity of the oak tree ultimately leads to its demise, just as a rigid mind or attitude can keep you from learning and growing and thereby lead to stress and discontent over time. If you cannot be pliable in your thinking or your response to a situation, then you have limited your options for success, for growth, and for joy. So how can we remain pliable and responsive and centered? We already know that one main ingredient is being present and aware of what is happening so that you *can* respond flexibly. Let's take a look at a martial analogy.

Most literally, the combative arts require one to be fully present and fluid in order to not get caught flat-footed and knocked off balance—or knocked out! You have to respond to the punch coming in order to avoid or block it. Yip Man encouraged young Bruce to train hard and then to forget about himself and instead follow his opponent's movements. To be like water is to adapt in response to your environment and your opponent. In other words, it is to be pliable.

But how does this concept apply more broadly to living life? Being like water means to be "in flow": first, be present and aware, then adaptable and mobile. In life, wouldn't being able to maintain awareness in order to then flow around your problems be helpful when navigating what life throws at you? Though my father never explicitly used the more modern term "flow state," he talked about "flowing" often. For him, being like water expanded far beyond a metaphor for gung fu to become a guiding philosophy for all of life—one that he applied to learning new things, overcoming obstacles, and, ultimately, finding his true path.

My father used the notion of living water as his approach. I say "living water" because we're not talking about stagnant pools, just as we're not talking about cultivating a stagnant life. My father used the concept of the flowing stream or the waves in the ocean often in his writings. As my father said, "Like flowing water, life is perpetual movement."

Life is always in motion. It is never set. Even within our daily, concretized routines, there are subtle differences at play—our timing, our mood, our environment. Today you get out the door five minutes early; tomorrow you have a headache; you just had a fight with a friend; maybe it's raining; or maybe you just fell in love. One day is never truly like the next, so to approach each day like it's the same and not constantly changing and fluctuating (i.e., in motion) would mean not being present or conscious of our full experience, and thereby not being able to be fluid in response to our subtly shifting lives. Many factors affect us and alter our responses and reactions to even the most basic of our routines, so to create hard and fast rules or assumptions about how we live or about how life should be can get us into trouble fast, especially when life decides to throw us a curveball.

In the words of Greek philosopher Heraclitus, "No man ever steps in the same river twice, for it's not the same river and he's not the same man." Each day, we are different, and circumstances are different. Even when a situation you have encountered before appears to be the same, it's not. Nothing is constant. There are always subtleties at play. The complexity of life means that every single moment and situation and challenge is new, maybe only slightly so, but still worthy of your presence and pliability nonetheless.

When my father created his martial art of jeet kune do (JKD), he took great care to establish deep philosophical principles to accompany it. These philosophies were meant to engage the mind and the spirit as well as the body and were a key component to guarding against rote drilling and perfunctory training. JKD emphasizes formlessness and non-telegraphic movement—movement that happens so instantaneously and in perfect response to the actual situation that the opponent cannot see what's coming. The philosophy attached to JKD is meant to root the practitioner in a fluid and present state to keep him or her flexible and capable of initiating and responding to change. And one can only respond to change if one has enough mobility in approach to do so.

> Every action should have its why and wherefore. I wish
> to infuse the spirit of philosophy into martial arts;

therefore I insist on studying philosophy. Philosophy brings my jeet kune do into a new realm in the sphere of martial arts!

Though he started ideating the art in 1965 (not formally naming it until 1967), he struggled throughout his life to leave behind his ideas in some lasting form, such as a book. He failed to publish his ideas precisely because he thought of his art as a living thing capable of change and evolution and did not want practitioners to believe that what was written down was the extent of it. (On this count, I definitely relate!) He worried they would not bring their unique experience to the process of learning. He struggled so much with it that though he took many technique photos and wrote pages upon pages of text about his thoughts on combat, he could never bring himself to publish them, wanting to avoid the problem of concretization and creating "devout" followers who would refuse to question their own experience.

That said, the book *Tao of Jeet Kune Do* was published posthumously in 1975 by my mother and Mito Uyehara of *Black Belt* magazine to attempt to preserve the teachings and thoughts of my father in the wake of his passing. Great care was taken to create a book that was not a mechanical how-to manual, but rather something that would make the reader think and explore for themselves, proving once again just how ingrained it was for Bruce Lee's friends and family to remain true to his wish to remain open and flexible in all approaches. Other "how-to" books later followed, but the *Tao of Jeet Kune Do* remains the quintessential book on the subject, even if it is the most abstract. And it is exactly this level of abstraction in its presentation that makes it so beautifully reflect my father's water principles: because in seeking to guide the reader, it doesn't seek to bind the reader, but rather allow the reader to be an active and flexible participant in their own process of understanding.

Have Appropriate Tension

One of the first teachings of jeet kune do is the on-guard position:

> The on-guard position is that position most favorable to
> the mechanical execution of all the total techniques and
> skills. It allows complete relaxation, yet, at the same
> time, gives a muscle the tension most favorable to quick
> reaction time. The on-guard position must, above all,
> be a "proper spiritual attitude" stance.
>
> —FROM THE *TAO OF JEET KUNE DO* BY BRUCE LEE

The "on-guard position" was what my father called the starting
stance for his art—the position from which all movement should ig-
nite whenever possible. His stance was very unique. It was based on
his understanding of the laws of physics and biomechanics, as well
as an assessment of many combative arts—wing chun, boxing, and
fencing chief among them.

Bruce Lee's on-guard position was both relaxed yet active. In this
position, the rear heel is raised like a coiled serpent, ready to push off
and strike at a moment's notice. The limbs are loose but not floppy.
The knees bent, the feet hip-width apart, about the distance of a natural step between them, the back toe pointed at the front foot's instep,
forming a triangle of stability, making it hard to knock you backward
or side to side. In other words, active yet stable, relaxed but ready.

If you watch my dad in his films, he is often bouncing around
loosely in front of his opponent in his signature way. He is light on his
feet. Ready to spring forward, sidestep, fall back, or cut the angle at any
moment. But he stays in an approximation of the above stance even
in movement so that he can strike instantly.

He writes about his stance: "Fundamental positioning is the

foundation." And so, I proffer, it is with an approach to life. A good foundation means having a strong posture that is able to adapt and move in any direction. It means just the right balance of relaxation and tension such that responses can be immediate and efficient. And it means being able to move and reposition simply and with ease so that you're never caught with your weight on your heels—"a simple and effective organization of oneself mentally and physically." This is a posture for engaged living.

When you think about it, water is always relaxed but ready. Think about the phrase "opening the floodgates." When the water is being held back by an obstruction of some kind, it is calmly waiting but ready to move. Remove the obstruction, and the water comes rushing through immediately without a moment's hesitation. Even while moving, it is in complete and effortless response to its environment. Throw a log across a moving stream and the water adapts. It will spread and widen and deepen and work on any cracks or fissures it can until it finds a way through or creates an ecosystem all around and within. Water is responsive and alive.

In order for water to be so "on-guard," it has to be holding a certain amount of tension. We tend to think of the word *tension* as a negative thing—tension in our neck and shoulders, tension in a relationship. But actually tension is a necessary component to aliveness. In order to metaphorically adapt an "on-guard" position in life, we need to strike a balance of aliveness. We don't need to be overly tense so as to be straining, but we also can't be so relaxed that we are checked out and incapable of responding. We need there to be a level of alertness that is grounded in a personal desire to be involved in our own lives. We need a modicum of appropriate tension—enough that we are present, pliable, and engaged, such that when the floodgates open, we can flow on through.

Be Purposeful

One of the burning questions we all have is: "What is my purpose?" What am I meant to be doing with this life? What mark am I meant to leave? What's my most important work? What is this all for anyway? My father would say the most important work you have in life is to be yourself, or, as he called it: to self-actualize. *What* you do (teach, play sports, feed starving children, enforce the laws, write books) and *who* you are (a parent, a spouse, a partner, a mentor, an artist) is not as important as *how* you express your "what" and your "who" in everything you do. How are you being? This is what people mean when they use the word *embodiment*. To embody an idea, a practice, a value, or a concept is to integrate it into your being, which is expressed through your doing. To say that kindness is important to you, but then not to be kind means you have not fully embodied the value of kindness.

To self-actualize is to raise your human vibration, reach for your greatest potential, and express it outwardly as you move through life at the highest level possible, whatever that may be. Where you choose to express it—in your hobbies, in your work, in your relationships—is just the vehicle through which you shine your light. When your purpose is simply to be the most high-functioning and joyful version of you that you can be, then every moment can be an opportunity to fulfill your purpose, and the journey becomes so much more exciting. You now have your purpose no matter what. Even the difficulties become more manageable when we are committed to expressing the truth of who we are.

My father encouraged a lifelong process of *self-actualization*. To actualize means "to make a reality of," and so then to *self*-actualize is to make a reality of oneself. It is to know oneself and express the uniqueness of oneself in the world with such skill and with such ease that, like water, it will flow naturally from you. Think about how water is water—it doesn't try to be anything else. To be like water is to be engaged in a process of discovering and then embodying our most real and true selves.

Sounds easy, right? Yes, but as you start down the path to self-knowledge and discovery, you may come to realize how much you are not being true to yourself, and maybe not even to the people around you. And suddenly you may realize, "Uh-oh. This is hard! I don't like this." But, as with everything, you don't get to be Bruce Lee by taking one kung fu class. You don't get to be a concert pianist in one lesson. And you don't get to express your best self out in the world without a healthy dose of personal inventory and integrity. It takes work to make your insides match your outsides.

When we're born, we are naturally open, sensing, responsive, energetic little beings, but as we are taught to navigate the world, we start to *try* to be one way or another, and our essence can get bogged down by the influence of so many other people and what they believe is right for us. Part of this programming is the normal, natural process of growing up and learning about the world, seeing that there are rules for survival and learning how to navigate them. We need to know how to protect ourselves, how to get what we need, and how to get by. But in this process, we also become separated from our essential selves by outside influence. As we learn how to conform, we can forget how to advocate for our uniqueness. We can forget how to naturally be and how to give voice and expression to our soul. And so we have to become aware and vigilant as we develop, and we have to practice our return to self until we finally reclaim with consciousness what we had in our possession all along: our free, expressive, and essential nature.

Water doesn't have this problem. A wave doesn't have to remember how to land on the shore. A river doesn't have to consider how to carve a canyon into a mountain. A lake doesn't have to practice giving life to the fish and the plants. In its simple way of just being, water can be our guide along our path to our natural selves. And one day, if we self-actualize, we can attain (and reclaim) this simple and natural freedom.

Be Whole

Yin yang was very important to my father. He used yin yang in the symbol he created for his martial art. He was very well versed in the philosophy of yin yang. Whole books, movements, and schools have grown up around the understanding and embodying of yin yang, and we will talk more about it as we go, but for now, let's start with a basic understanding of the symbol as a representation for wholeness.

In the Western world, we tend to consider yin and yang as opposites: hot and cold, young and old, tall and short. But in the Eastern world, yin yang (notice I removed the *and* separating the two) are considered complements of one another, not opposites. In fact, they work together to represent the whole of experience. If you think about it, hot and cold are merely the extreme ends of the whole experience of temperature. Without hot, there is not cold, and vice versa. And further, without both, there is not the moderate pleasantness of warmth or coolness.

And so it is with water. Water is gentle yet powerful. Soft, yet strong. Flowing, yet deep. And so it is with life. Life can be joyful and sad. Beautiful and ugly. Exciting and terrifying. And yet, these are the extremes of the whole experience. If we resist one half of the experience, we may never reach the heights of its rewards or the contentment of its balance. But when we strike a balance within the interplay of these extremes, we find peace and harmony. We find ease.

So let us seek the full experience of this thing we call our life. Let's look at the entire ecosystem of our being and our humanity. And let's remember that, like water, we can flow quickly or slowly. We can train hard while being gentle with ourselves in the process. The journey of flowing toward self-actualization and wholeness is not undertaken lightly. It will require your full attention. But as you grow, you will begin to see and, more important, to experience a fluid interplay between the elements that make *you* you. As my father wrote in a philosophical essay:

> The Chinese conceived the entire universe as activated by two principles, the Yang and the Yin, the positive and the negative. And they considered that nothing that exists, either animate or so-called inanimate, does so except by the ceaseless interplay of these two forces. Yang and Yin, Matter and Energy, Heaven and Earth are conceived of as essentially One, or as two coexistent poles of one indivisible whole. It is a philosophy of the essential unity of the universe and eternal cycles, of the leveling of all differences, the relativity of standards, and the return of all to the divine intelligence, the source of all things.

So now that we have our toe in the vast pond of the universe, let's go a little deeper. Come on in—the water is fine. . . .

2

The Empty Cup

The usefulness of a cup is in its emptiness.

Empty Your Mind

In an article my father wrote in 1971 about his art of jeet kune do, he started off with a Zen parable to prepare the reader to keep an open mind, as what he was about to go on to say was extremely unorthodox for fighting arts of the time. He wrote:

> A learned man once went to a Zen master to inquire about Zen. As the master talked, the learned man would frequently interrupt him with remarks like, "Oh yes, we have that too," and so forth. Finally, the Zen master stopped talking and began to serve tea to the learned man; however, he kept pouring, and the tea cup

overflowed. "Enough! No more can go into the cup!" the learned man interrupted. "Indeed, I see," answered the Zen master. "If you do not first empty your cup, how can you taste my cup of tea?"

The "learned" man can't truly take in anything that the Zen master is saying because he is simultaneously comparing and judging the information against his own. In other words, he's not really listening. His mind (his cup) is too full of his own point of view (measuring and evaluating everything the master has to say) to let anything else in. In overflowing the cup, the master shows the man how he must let go of that which he already thinks he knows—he must empty his cup—in order to really listen and take in new information.

The "Be Water" quote begins with the prompt, "Empty your mind." This first request is perhaps the most important one in our process because it sets us up for everything that comes next. My father believed that this act—of leaving behind the burdens of one's preconceived opinions and conclusions—had in itself a liberating power. In fact, if this step is the only one you actively work on for a while, you will expand your life considerably.

Finding Neutrality

Emptiness, in these first discussions on the mind, means a state of openness and neutrality. When your mind is crowded with thoughts and information about all the things you've learned and how you feel about them, there isn't room for much else. You've given up access to new possibilities and points of view; you've limited yourself. In order to learn new information, we must first make room to let that information in.

Emptying your mind does not mean forgetting everything you've ever learned or giving up everything you believe. What it means is that you should try to meet each conversation, each interaction, and each experience with a willingness to consider something new without the burden of your judgment in the process. You must give up everything you think you know and believe, for just an instant, in order to fully experience that which you are encountering in the present moment. Make room for the possibility that maybe you don't already know all of what you believe to be true—that what you believe is, in fact, a work in progress, capable of changing and evolving as you learn and grow.

It is under these conditions that you may discover something that you never thought was possible. Take the medical profession, for example: if we never considered there might be new information or ideas, we would still believe that smoking was good for you and that polio was incurable. So this is a serious idea: that the mind should stand open and unclouded by one's previously held preferences, beliefs, or judgments in order to be ready to receive. You may or may not end up discovering a new vaccine, but without being open to the possibility of what there is to discover, you'll never expand your knowledge, and your growth as a person will be stunted and slowed.

In fact, my father suggests that predetermined and unquestioned preferences are the mind's worst disease. "Stand at the neutral point between negative and positive," he wrote, "no longer directing one's mind to anything. Emptiness is that which stands right in the middle of this and that. Never be for or against. The struggle between 'for' and 'against' is the mind's worst disease. Do not like or dislike, and all will then be clear."

Consider how much influence your preferences and beliefs have on you in every moment of every day. As we go through our day, we are expert evidence collectors—so much so that we should all have our own *CSI* show. Because of our beliefs and our preferences, we walk around collecting the evidence of our experiences to bolster our beliefs. If

I walk into a party with a sense of dread, then I am subconsciously looking for evidence of that dread to prove myself right. And it may be true that there are things to dread at the party, but because I'm on high alert for all the dreadfulness, I will conveniently find it and *not* see anything that might be enjoyable or fun. We are always looking to be proved right. And when we have a need to be right, we will only accept that which substantiates our point of view.

And what happens when we can't collect that evidence? When our case isn't lining up so well? Well, if the experience is enjoyable when we're expecting otherwise (like that party that turned out to be not so bad after all), then we brush it off as a pleasant anomaly or we just feel like we got lucky. But when the experience we thought would be great turns out to be not so pleasant, well, then suddenly the world seems incomprehensible. Let's say a party you really believed would be amazing ends up being a nightmare experience instead. It's wounding, and we decide we are never going to another party like that. Interestingly, when something negative happens against our expectation, instead of thinking that there may be something more to consider or some personal responsibility to shoulder, most of us decide that we are victims of something more sinister than we had previously known—a universal plot to ruin our lives.

But what if you went into that party with no expectations? No sense of dread and no expectation of having the time of your life? Then the party just is what it is. You can assess for yourself later what parts of it you really enjoyed and what parts you didn't. You met each moment of the party as it occurred. No stress. Your full attention is on the party without having to constantly check with yourself if you're having a good enough time. Neutral. Present. Empty.

Of course, when it comes to functions we may or may not want to attend, the stakes aren't so high. But what about when it comes to more charged and serious topics? What about difficult life choices that need to be made? Or making judgments between people who might be good for us versus bad influences? If we are never for or against anything, how do we make decisions?

Choiceless Awareness

Remember the on-guard position? Our poised and ready posture in the face of any situation? Let's consider that the mental version of our opening stance on life should be this one of poised neutrality. What we are trying to cultivate is what my father called the ability to see purely. "Pure seeing" means to try, as much as possible, not to project one's preferences or opinions onto something in the process of experiencing it, so that what you encounter is the "truth" or the reality of things as they are in their objective totality. Instead of weighing everything as good or bad, right or wrong, as it is happening, become a fully sensing organism so that you may see and encounter the experience with your whole being. If you focus too much on the mind and its preconceived ideas and assessments, you are holding part of yourself separate from the totality of the experience. But if you can pause and allow yourself to sense everything, perhaps you will experience something new or a richer version of something you already know.

> It is to see things as they are and not become attached to anything. Scratch away all the dirt our being has accumulated and reveal reality in its is-ness, in its nakedness. Drop the burden of your preconceived conclusions and "open" yourself to everything and everyone ahead. Be a calm beholder of what is happening around you. You simply see, and in this seeing, the whole is presented and not the partial.

This is a process my father called "choiceless awareness." He adopted this term from Krishnamurti, one of his favorite philosophers. The idea is to have awareness of all that is happening around you and within you without judging it, without making a choice or creating a story about it while maintaining full awareness of it. See it purely for what it is. Experience it fully so that you can have a total experience rather than a partial (and therefore limited) one.

Consider the situation when you see someone who annoys you coming over to talk to you. Because that person annoys you, you are prepared to be annoyed before they even open their mouths. But what if you were to drop your judgment and open yourself fully to the experience? Perhaps in having the ability to just stand back and observe this person without judgment, you might pinpoint what it is that annoys you so much, and you might go even further and figure out *why* that annoys *you*. And, more important, you might find out something about yourself in the process.

Is there some understanding you need to develop within yourself to feel good or safe or connected in this person's presence? Can you have compassion for this person and see them as someone who is struggling through life just as you are? Can you see how their own set of circumstances has led them to develop this way of interacting as their cultivated method of coping? A great amount of information might be available if you stop liking and disliking and simply observe.

Another part of the choiceless awareness equation is what my father called "absence of thought." Absence of thought means not to be carried away by your thoughts in the process of thinking them. In other words, don't get stuck on a particular thought and spin around it obsessively to the detriment of all the other sensory input that passes through your perception in the moment. So when the annoying person does that annoying thing, don't get stuck there. "See? There is that annoying thing again. God, why does he do that all the time? Doesn't he see how annoying that is? How could he not see how annoying that is? What an idiot." When this happens, you are no longer present. You are trapped in a box of annoyance from which there is no escape, and you are no longer seeing purely, and you are certainly not having a nonjudgmental awareness of the whole situation. And guess what: you're no longer having a good time, either.

Now, this doesn't mean you have to spend time in annoying situations with annoying people and learn to like it. It simply means you get the opportunity to have a different experience and change your perspective. Most notably, you get to use the information you receive to know yourself better and understand what your biases are or what triggers certain reactions in you. You get to assess what behaviors need to be changed in yourself and what parts of yourself may need to be healed. In other words, you get to convert that negative energy into energy for yourself rather than give it all away to someone or something else.

As my father said:

> I must give up my desire to force, direct, strangle the world outside of me and within me in order to be completely open, responsible, aware, alive. This is often called "to make oneself empty," which does not mean something negative, but means the openness to receive.

From this place, we can make the decisions we need to while understanding ourselves and what might truly be in line with our soul. We will also have more compassion and acceptance of what is. From this place, we have so much more possibility.

No Right, No Wrong

We are judgy f*cks. Let's just admit it. Maybe you are currently trying not to be so judgmental in your life, and if so, good. But you still catch yourself doing it sometimes, don't you? Me too. But the more I practice not judging, the better I get at maintaining this nonjudgmental attitude, and the more freely and peaceably I can navigate the world.

What does it mean to be judgmental? It means to assign a value of right or wrong, good or bad, like or dislike to something or someone. How does this hold us back? Well, first let's distinguish between judgment and discernment.

A "judgment," in the most traditional sense, means a conclusion or decision, as by a court or a judge. The oldest form of judgment comes from the Bible and typically refers to a storm or a plague sent by God to punish people. Heavy, right? But "discernment" is less of a conclusion and more of a process: it's the ability to make valuable perceptions about something. One spiritual definition even calls discernment "perception in the absence of judgment with a view to obtaining spiritual direction and understanding." (source unknown)

When we need to make decisions in life, there are, of course, considerations to take into account—but the approach we take makes all the difference. When we're judging, we're taking a rigid position; whereas when we're discerning, we're perceiving with the goal of understanding. A judgment holds us back because it limits our consideration of other options. It also pits us against one another, because if something or someone is right, then that means someone is also wrong. But a discernment is a choice made for oneself based on all the available data without blame.

The difference between judgment and discernment may be hard to see right away, but practice asking yourself: "Am I judging right now? Or am I allowing information in with the goal of understanding what is really going on and how I really feel?" As you become more aware, you'll be able to feel the difference between the two. A judgment may feel like a hard line running through you or like a shield that keeps things away from you. A discernment may feel more like water washing over you while you pan for gold—there's a porousness, a fluidity as you sift through the information.

One of my favorite books is *The Four Agreements* by Don Miguel Ruiz, a quick and beautiful read with great practical impact. *The Four Agreements* deals specifically with dropping your assumptions and not taking things personally. What do you need to do in order to achieve those two things? As Ruiz suggests in the title of his book, you must make certain agreements with yourself about how to encounter the world. And as my father suggests, you need to stop making everything and everyone right or wrong:

> Do not condemn; do not justify. To truly understand there must be a state of choiceless awareness in which there is no sense of comparison or condemnation, no waiting for a further development of the thing we are talking about in order to agree or disagree. Awareness only works if it is allowed free play without interference. Above all, don't start from a conclusion.

When you are "waiting for a further development in order to agree or disagree," you are waiting to judge based on a personal assumption or belief you already have and that you are looking to defend. You are looking for the evidence of the judgment you hold. Remember the man and the Zen master? Your cup is too full. Your awareness is being squeezed into the limited framework of your comparison or your condemnation. You are no longer in flowing discernment; rather, you are waiting for the moment to pounce with your judgment. Does that feel good—waiting to pounce? Or does it feel stressful? Like you're the goalie waiting tensely to block a penalty kick at all times?

In his book *A New Earth*, Eckhart Tolle says, "The primary cause of unhappiness is never the situation but your thoughts about it. Be aware of the thoughts you are thinking. Separate them from the situation, which is always neutral, which always is as it is."

Similarly, my father submits that it is our reaction to difficult situations that matters most, and not the situation itself.

> Believe me that in every big thing or achievement there are always obstacles, big or small, and the reaction one shows to such obstacles is what counts, not the obstacle itself. I have learned that being challenged means one thing and that is what is your reaction to it?

Let's go back to a fight as our best example. You come into the fight cocky and sure that you will win. That confidence even fuels some pretty sweet moves on your part for a minute. Then you get hit in the face. Maybe you get upset. Maybe your confidence gets a little rocked. Either way, you feel something. And instead of just allowing that feeling to pass through you and staying present with the situation, you let that feeling take you over. Now you're mad or worried. So you react accordingly. Maybe you overreach with your swing in your anger or you get tentative in your strikes out of fear. If your opponent is on their game, they can see they've gotten to you and now they have their way in. They slip in a kick to the thigh because you were distracted and no longer present. Uh-oh. This isn't going as you envisioned it. You start to make mistakes because you are ungrounded and spinning into anxiety. Reality is no longer matching your preconceived plan. Your opponent lands one more heavy hand, and now it's lights-out.

You came into the fight with a foregone conclusion—I'm going to win; I'm better than them. Then you got hit and it rocked you and you stopped being present with the fight. Your mind got hung up, trapped, and couldn't stay with it. Then your fear kicked in and all that training, all your tools, became useless because you were no longer there to use them. You got attached to what "should have happened," and when that didn't transpire, you were lost.

But no need to condemn yourself when that occurs. People get lost; it happens. And the goal is to try not to be lost any longer than it takes to be found again. After all, there is no right or wrong; there's only what is happening and your response. So stop trying to come up with a magic one-size-fits-all solution. There is no flawless, preconceived road map for life. Within all our grand notions and ideas, there is only ever the right here and the right now.

What Is

We touched on presence in chapter one, and we likely will again and again throughout this book because it's an important concept. Whole books have been written about just this one topic. Whole movements, such as mindfulness, are about being present. And our empty cup, our neutral but mobile stance, begins with presence as well.

If you are new to the idea of mindfulness or being present, let me try to set a simple framework for our purposes in this moment. The idea of being present is the idea of being fully aware and in touch with what's happening *right now*. Not letting your mind, for example, jump into the past to compare what you are doing right now to a similar thing you did last year. And not jumping ahead into the future and thinking about what you're going to do this afternoon or next week or thinking about how what you're experiencing now will benefit you later. The practice of mindfulness is focusing one's awareness on the present moment and experiencing it fully.

Because we are human, and particularly if we are not practiced at staying present, thoughts are going to pop up to distract us from the present moment. And those thoughts may lead to feelings or vice versa. And those feelings may generate more thoughts about the feelings. This is normal. In fact, it may never have occurred to you that any other way of being was possible. So rather than try to beat down our thoughts and feelings, which gives them more power, we want to merely *notice* them, allow them, and let them pass through as we stay with the present moment.

The notion of emptying your cup is the idea of letting go of the past and the future in favor of the present. When we gently accept and acknowledge feelings, thoughts, and bodily sensations while participating in what is happening, we are in touch with what my father called "what is." We are participating in what is unfolding right now with our full attention. And we want to continually empty the cup as it is filled because the present moment is always changing. So if we stay with the present moment, our cup will automatically fill and empty as we move across our experience—each new moment replaced with each new moment.

Now, if this seems like a tall order, it is, at first. And it's nearly impossible to be fully present at every moment for most of us, so don't panic. Not even very capable Buddhists or yogis are present 24/7. This is a practice, and it requires practice. The point of the practice is to be able to bring yourself back to it whenever possible and especially in times of great distress, so that presence becomes the majority of your experience and not the anomaly.

My father was not always successful at maintaining his awareness and his cool, but he understood the benefits. In fact, he was a fiery, fast-paced, driven man who could have a temper. When things didn't work out or when he hadn't approached a situation with the utmost of awareness, what would he do? He would get upset! Which is the normal human response. Then, after he felt all the feels, he would get really quiet for a while. This purposeful quieting is what I like to think of as his "emptying the cup" moment. He would quiet his mind to get back to a neutral state in order to see the whole picture before moving forward again, like the little pooling swirls and eddies in a stream that form and spin around before the water flows forth once more.

Mental Kung Fu

So, how do we get to neutral? My father was an exercise fanatic, as we can clearly see from his physique, and an important part of his exercise routine was exercising not just his body but his mind. Though we tend to think of our amorphous mental calculations and ponderings as somehow separate from our physical bodies, scientific research continues to provide compelling evidence of the mind-body connection and the link between our thoughts and emotions to our physical health. There's been a lot of research especially around the gut-brain connection, and even an entire field of research called psychoneuroimmunology, which examines the link between stress and the immune system—but let's take a more general approach we can all relate to.

One simple way to understand the mind-body connection is to notice that when we have negative thoughts, we feel bad; we feel heavy or tired or agitated, our hearts might race, or we might have trouble falling asleep or getting out of bed in the morning, or we just feel blue. In other words, our bodies respond. Likewise, when we are joyful, we have more energy; we feel good! We get more done; we laugh. There's a clear correlation; and as a result, we must consider the benefit of conditioning our minds with the same understanding that we have around conditioning our bodies.

And in fact, our minds are already conditioned—by what we read, how we were raised, what culture we are part of, who we hang out with, what we study, etc. We just may not be conscious of the conditioning we've undergone and we may not understand that we have any part to play in this conditioning. What if we came to understand that we have some control here and can, in fact, direct and recondition our minds toward new possibilities instead of remaining unconscious or ignorant of its workings? What if we could work in collaboration with our minds rather than be at the mercy of our thoughts? What if negative could be converted to positive? What if fear could be transformed into enthusiasm? What if mistakes could become the pathways to our dreams?

My father focused just as much energy on conditioning his mind as he did on training his body. That doesn't mean, though, that he got into calculus, crossword puzzles, or sudoku. Instead he intentionally directed his thoughts, his intellect, and his imagination toward his dreams, toward the life that he imagined, toward the goals he hoped to achieve, toward positivity, and toward understanding himself better. He concertedly conditioned his consciousness and subconscious, and deliberately stretched his mental muscles so he could change his attitude to be more pliable and expand his perception in the direction of his goals.

He had many tools at his disposal, which we will touch on throughout this book. But this mental conditioning (or reconditioning) begins by preparing your mind to be open to receive—clearing out all the mental clutter and noise, turning off the inner dialog, and stepping firmly into the present with all your judgments suspended and all your sensors turned up.

This mental reconditioning may sound daunting or it may sound easy, but it's both and neither. As with anything, it requires practice until it becomes habit, and then eventually the habit becomes second nature. So how to start?

First, we must accept the idea that it's possible to exercise our own mental leadership. We must agree that we can command and cultivate our own minds.

If you are struggling with this notion, then let me remind you that you have learned many things by repetition and reinforcement. This is likely how you learned your multiplication tables; you probably also learned not to interrupt people who are talking by being constantly reminded by your parents not to do so. You have been taught or self-taught many things, such as how to speak another language or how to follow a recipe.

Still, so many of us feel as if we have no control over our thoughts and feelings, and hence, our attitudes. Maybe we've never stopped to consider that we may be abdicating this control and responsibility altogether. So take this leap with me and let's acknowledge that we have personal power over our mental conditioning if we want it. This is the first major step in the journey to discover and maximize your human potential. And that first major step starts with this small one: What are thinking about right now?

The Sticky Mind

Do you notice your thoughts? Are you aware of what you think? Can you easily hear your inner dialogue? Take a moment to stop and listen to yourself think. Notice how the dialogue can morph and change course very easily, especially once you pay attention to it. Notice how some of your thoughts are very practical and solution oriented, such as "I have to pick up my dry cleaning," while some of them are judgmental of yourself or others, such as "I'm an idiot for forgetting to pay my gas bill." Some of them are pleasant and kind—"I look great in this outfit"—and some of them are just plain weird: "I wonder what it feels like to freeze to death." Listening in on the dialogue of your own mind is the first step toward being aware of (and ultimately cultivating) what is in your cup.

As you practice listening to your thoughts, see if you can start to notice where your mind gets stuck. What thoughts do you return to again and again? What ideas begin to sound like a broken record? Do you tell yourself you're stupid over and over? Do you constantly look at what other people are wearing or how they look and compare yourself to them? Do you see people creating great works of art and long to create art of your own? Do you wish you were doing something else, or were at some different point in your life, but you don't know what or where?

There have been periods in my life where I've been stuck on all sorts of comparisons and negativity. If someone I know was in love and having a beautiful relationship while I was single, my thoughts could run the gambit from envy to self-pity to hopelessness around ever being loved. Rather than just being happy for my friend, remaining open to finding love, and feeling good, my mind would get stuck on why I was not in a relationship, as if I could think my way into a relationship if only I could figure it out (whatever "it" is).

My father called this the "grasping mind" or "sticky mind." In martial arts, it refers to a moment in an encounter where you get stuck trying to enforce some strategy you may have that's separate from what is actually happening in the present moment. You become too clever and jammed up with your training or your game plan or your emotions, and you stop responding to the moment as it actually unfolds. In other words, you get in your own way. Sound familiar?

I was watching a UFC fight once, and while they were doing the short pre-fight intro pieces for each fighter before the match, one of the fighters started talking about his fight plan and how he was going to first do this and then do that and then win by doing this. He was being very specific about it, and I thought to myself, *That guy is going to lose.* And he did. He lost because he got too caught up in what he wanted the fight to be, rather than what the fight actually was. And when the fight started to deviate from his plan, he didn't have enough flow, presence, maturity, and ability to respond appropriately in the moment and change course to alter the outcome. His mind was stuck in what he'd predetermined and hoped or assumed would happen, and he was unable to see, perceive, and respond to what was actually happening. He wasn't present. His cup was too full.

> Have a mind that has no dwelling place but continues to flow ceaselessly and ignores our limitations and our distinctions. Do not strive to localize the mind anywhere but let it fill up the whole body; let it flow freely throughout the totality of your being. Do not let the mind be grasping or sticky. Don't look at "what is" from the position of thinking what should be. It is not to be without emotion or feeling but to be one in whom feeling is not sticky or blocked.

That bears repeating: "It is not to be without emotion or feeling but to be one in whom feeling is not sticky or blocked." It is not to deny or bury or go around your feelings or your thoughts about those feelings. It is to feel them, acknowledge them, and work with them—to understand what they are trying to tell you about you, about the situation—to let them show you where there is more work to be done without letting them overwhelm, unbalance, or trap you. They have information for you. Take the information, say thank you, and keep going.

Meditation as a Tool

It may come as no surprise that my father meditated, starting as a teenager and continuing throughout the rest of his life in one form or another. Meditation is a great tool for creating that calm space in the mind that is needed to gain perspective and to empty your cup. I know many people who meditate regularly, and I know many people who just can't take to it. The truth is, everyone meditates in some form— you just may not realize that you already know how. My father did occasionally sit, legs crossed, eyes closed, palms resting comfortably in his lap to meditate, but he engaged in other types of meditation as well. But before we get to that, let's talk about why meditation might be useful.

For our purposes in this moment, meditation should be understood as a method of loosening the mind and letting it float a bit. It's a practice of creating space—freeing yourself from all motives and

helping you to make contact with your relaxed and serene nature. You can think of it as the feeling you have when you daydream. You're awake, but your mind is untethered and moving easily from image to idea to thought and through states of nothingness, without getting hung up on any one thing—like it's floating in a gentle and deep pool of water with inflatable water wings on. It doesn't need to do anything to stay afloat. It feels loose; it feels free. No "thoughts" as we traditionally think of them are getting any active play. You aren't thinking about your day or your to-do list or the argument you had with your partner or where you have to be after you're done meditating. You're not in evidence-collecting mode. You simply give yourself the space to let go of thinking at all.

Of course, and especially in the beginning, nagging thoughts do grab our attention when trying to meditate. One of the mind's main functions is analysis, and so it's normal and natural for the mind to shift quickly back to problem-solving and planning. When that happens, don't beat yourself up or get frustrated. It's part of the process, and, in fact, the mere act of noticing that this has occurred is a huge step in the right direction. It means you're becoming aware! So just notice when this happens, pat yourself on the back, and then pump up your water wings and bring your focus back to neutral.

There are many techniques for establishing this space of calm. Some people follow the breath in and out, directing the mind back to the breath when it starts to wander or judge the experience (which it invariably will). Some people use mantras or visualizations. My father liked to meditate a little differently for the most part. He often liked to untether his mind and let it float while he was moving, surprise, surprise. He used his morning jog as meditative time. He sometimes would also walk around our backyard while simultaneously meditating. It's not about how you do it—whether your eyes are open or closed, whether you are sitting or moving—it's about that space of mental calm. It's about the untethering and making room for new perceptions. And figuring out how that works for you is another step toward understanding yourself and how your cup best empties.

I want us to consider this type of meditation as a potential tool in our tool belt for practicing the art of being like water. My father was very certain that meditation should not be about "striving" to be still and calm. "Striving" is the antithesis of being empty. When he was a young man, my father wrote about the cognitive dissonance we often experience in meditation:

> "I must relax." But then I had just thought something that contradicted my will at the precise moment I thought, "I must relax." The demand for effort in *must* was already inconsistent with the effortlessness in *relax*.

In meditation, we should allow, surrender, loosen, let go. Just make space and embody space.

The practices of mindfulness and meditation are similar in that they bring you back to the now. And they are both excellent techniques for learning to empty our cup. If you practice them daily, even just for five minutes, or while you are engaged in any activity that doesn't require you to think (jogging, coloring, walking, even washing dishes), you will start to develop a sense of energized relaxation, and there will suddenly be more room in your cup for all sorts of new possibilities. Just like my father on the boat when he was a teenager, you are giving yourself the space to ponder and feel and be.

One quick practice I like to do is just to take the first phrase of my father's "Be Water" quote and use it as a guided visualization toward quieting my mind and making space. I picture my mind like a sacred bowl filled with all my thoughts and feelings of the day, and as I say or think the words "Empty your mind; be formless, shapeless like water," I picture all those thoughts emptying out and washing down through my body like a gentle waterfall. I let the worries, the to-do lists, and the stress just filter down through my being and drain into the earth. Then I sit quietly as the bowl of my mind refills with clean, clear, still water or white light or whatever feels good. You can also view your empty bowl as an invitation for it to fill with whatever you need to see or feel in that moment. The important thing is not to force a vision or a feeling. Just allow. And if nothing comes, then fill your bowl with clear water or light and wash it down your body once again. Feel yourself being nourished. Feel yourself as lighter. Breathe and relax and just take these minutes to empty out. This practice makes me think of this quote of my father's:

> Who is there that can make muddy waters clear? But if allowed to remain still, it will become clear of itself. Who is there that can secure a state of absolute repose? But keep calm and let time go on, and the state of repose will gradually arrest.

Emptiness Is a Process

> We in the West think of nothingness as a void, a non-existence. In Eastern philosophy and modern physical science, nothingness—no-thingness—is a form of process, ever moving.

Remember that this foray into emptiness is a process. There's no way to achieve the end, because a process is ongoing. There is no end.

Once you start noticing your own inner dialog and practice emptying your mind of judgment, the process becomes part of you.

There will be times when you will forget about this practice altogether and fall back into old habits, and when that happens, simply start again. No need to admonish oneself for doing something "wrong." Our whole mission is to let go of that binary way of thinking that makes everything wrong or right. We can see what we've done or not done. We can see how we feel about it. It doesn't have to be wrong; it just is. As my father said:

> To live with "what is" is to be peaceful. There is "what is" when there is no comparison at all. Require not just a moment of perception, but a continuous awareness, a continuous state of inquiry in which there is no conclusion. Just watch choicelessly and in the watching lies the wonder. There is an awareness without any demand, an awareness in which there is no anxiety, and in that state of mind, there is perception. And it is perception that will resolve all our problems.

Can perception solve all our problems, as he says? In a lot of ways, yes. Perception may not be able to instantly materialize the money we need for rent tomorrow, but it may allow us to think of our situation differently and see possibilities where before we saw none. It may even help us to meet our challenges with a little more acceptance, calm, and poise than we could have before. And in that shift, there is huge potential for everything from tolerance to peace of mind to actual solutions showing up.

In most situations, if we can figure out how to see something in a new light, with a novel understanding, if we can learn something we didn't know about ourselves or about the situation, if we can drop our judgments, our expectations, and our rationalizations, and if we can learn to flow with and not resist our current circumstances, our cup can continually be filled with new possibilities, new answers, and new ideas—because there will always be more room. And then we can truly begin to transform our lives.

3

The Eternal Student

Life itself is your teacher,
and you are in a constant state of learning.

The Classical Mess

By 1964, my father had established his second martial arts school in Oakland, California. He was married to my mom, and they were expecting their first child, my brother, Brandon. My father's schools, in Seattle and now Oakland, called the Jun Fan Gung Fu Institutes, were teaching a slightly modified form of wing chun, the martial art he had learned in Hong Kong as a teenager. I say "slightly modified" because my father had started to contemplate and experiment with shifts in technique—these were very small deviations from the traditional norm, such as a slight angling of the foot here, more movement at the waist there, quicker initiation of movement in response to an opponent, etc. But for the most part, he was still teaching wing chun.

But because he was Bruce Lee and because he was twenty-four, he was a bit of a loudmouth. He was also bucking tradition in ways that annoyed the Chinese kung fu old guard in San Francisco's Chinatown community. My father would give demonstrations at the Sun Sing Theater in Chinatown, and he would talk loudly and brashly about how many of the Chinese martial arts were bogged down by unnecessary, wasted motions, using the term "classical mess" repeatedly to disparage other traditional kung fu styles. He would then challenge people to come up onstage and see if they could best his technique.

As if that weren't enough to ruffle feathers, he also opened his schools to people of all races and backgrounds. In the eyes of the kung fu establishment, traditions were meant to be adhered to, and while the occasional non-Chinese might find their way into Chinese kung fu classes from time to time, there was certainly not an open-door policy to the general public. Bruce was disrespectful and "ruining" the old ways, and for the traditionalists in Chinatown, this would not stand.

In late 1964, the San Francisco Chinatown community issued a challenge against my father. They'd had enough of this bold young man and his rebellious ways, and they were going to do what they could to silence him. They proposed a challenge match to be fought at my father's school in Oakland. If their champion won, Bruce Lee would cease teaching, and if my father won, he could continue on unimpeded. Of course, my father accepted the challenge. He was definitely not going to allow anyone to dictate his life in this way, and he was highly confident that he would be successful. He had faith in his ability, and there was no way he wasn't going to stand up for himself and his beliefs, no matter the outcome.

It may sound like something out of a movie, but this was real life for my family. My mother, who was several months pregnant at the time, was there for the fight, along with my father's good friend and assistant instructor James Lee (since deceased). The group from

Chinatown, which were several in number, assembled at my father's school in November of 1964 for the match. They presented their champion, a random fighter who they selected because of his prowess but who was not engaged in the matter directly, and then they began to lay down the rules. No eye gouging, no shots to the groin, no this, no that . . . This is where my father stopped them.

There would be no rules.

My father proclaimed that if they were indeed seeking to threaten his livelihood and attempt to shut down a very essential part of his being, then the match would have to be a real fight with nothing held back. The fight would end with a knockout or a submission. That was it. The Chinatown guys conferred briefly and agreed. Everyone moved to the side of the room, and without further ado, my father came out swinging.

The fight itself was very unorthodox. After the exchange of initial blows, the opponent took off running with my father trying to grab ahold of him and attack from the back. Traditional technique had taken a back seat to survival, and the blows were sloppy and a bit wild. The fight lasted all of about three minutes. My father's opponent ended up on his back, my father standing over him, fist poised, yelling in Cantonese, "Do you give up?! Do you give up?!" And finally, the man submitted and replied, "I give up."

After everyone had left, my father sat outside his school on the curb with his head in his hands like a defeated man, even though he had clearly won. My mother approached him and asked why he seemed upset. He should be celebrating, shouldn't he?

Yes, he had won. But he'd come away with something more powerful than the self-satisfaction of victory. Up to this point, when my father was giving demonstrations of his technique, he might say something like, "Try to hit me." Or "Try to block my punch." But those promptings were within the comfortable realm of his experience. That is to say, there was a certain level of expectation in what might happen in those scenarios; they were contained. But this fight had been different. It had tested him in a new way.

First of all, he'd had to chase this man around the room—not something you usually have to do in a fight—and he'd become winded. Secondly, he'd had to attack someone from the rear who was running away—also not something anyone practices in martial arts. And finally, they had done away with traditional stances, rules, and exchange of measured blows, and though my father had been the one to make this request, he still had not been totally prepared for what occurred.

The fight had shown him things about himself that he'd not previously known, particularly that he was not in great physical condition. Don't get me wrong; he was in fine shape, but he had attained that shape through the practicing of martial arts techniques only. He hadn't been cross-training or working on pure physical fitness. After the fight, he also saw clearly that his traditional wing chun training hadn't prepared him for an "anything goes" scenario. He had still won. He had kept his cool, and he'd delivered blows, but they'd been improvised and made him feel haphazard and out of control. He had seen how much more he had to consider and how much more he had to learn.

As it turns out, this fight would be a pivotal moment in my father's life. Had he not been "empty" enough to make room for a true assessment of the entire situation, he might have missed out on seeing all he had to learn. He could have high-fived his friend James, hugged my mom, gone out for a nice meal, and told his friends all about how he'd sent those old Chinatown guys packing. But then you probably wouldn't know his name today. And I certainly wouldn't be writing this book.

Instead of reveling in his victory, my father used the lessons of the fight to begin a long, personal journey. He became interested in

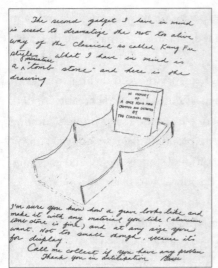

what it meant to be a well-rounded, physically fit, and fully creative fighter, what it meant to release oneself of limitations, and, most important for our purposes, what it meant to be a fluid human being.

Shortly after that fight, my father started to consider the physical realities of combat, and what might be possible when one wasn't bound by the traditions or norms of any particular style. This was the great revelation of his martial career, and the beginning of the art of jeet kune do. As a symbol and testament to his seriousness about this new journey, he reached out to metalworker, friend, and student George Lee and asked him to create something for him.

He sent George a sketch of a miniature tombstone and asked that the headstone read: *In memory of a once fluid man crammed and distorted by the classical mess*. This tombstone was my father's reminder that his limited, rigid, traditional approach must "die" in order for him to rise again as his original fluid self. It was a reminder to move forward like flowing water.

No Masters Allowed

Each man must seek out realization himself. No master
can give it to him.

My father never wanted to be called a master. He said, "Once you
say you've reached the top, then there is nowhere to go but down."
Instead he considered himself to be the eternal student—always open
to new ideas, new possibilities, new directions, and new growth.

He saw his process as the peeling of layers of a never-ending
onion—always uncovering new layers of his soul, and revealing new
levels of understanding:

> My life it seems is a life of self-examination: a self-
> peeling of myself, bit by bit, day by day. More and more
> it's becoming simple to me as a human being, more and
> more I search myself, and more and more the questions
> become listed. And more and more I see clearly. I am
> happy because I am growing daily and honestly don't
> know where my ultimate limit lies. To be certain, every
> day there can be a revelation or a new discovery that I
> can obtain.

These are the words of a man passionate about learning. This focused enthusiasm for understanding and growth lit him up and un-
leashed him. It gave him permission to explore and create and was a
hallmark of his genius. He made connections between disciplines and
ideas where others weren't even looking because he had an open mind
and was the consummate experimenter.

For instance, when it came to developing his art of jeet kune do, he
delved not just into standard martial arts for inspiration and information;

he looked at Western boxing, fencing, biomechanics, and philosophy. He admired the simplicity of boxing, incorporating its ideas into his footwork and his upper-body tools (jab, cross, hook, bob, weave, etc.). And from fencing, he began by looking at the footwork, range, and timing of the stop hit and the riposte, both techniques that meet attacks and defenses with preemptive moves. From biomechanics, he studied movement as a whole, seeking to understand the physical laws of motion while understanding biological efficiencies and strengths. And within philosophy, he read widely from both Eastern and Western writers, such as Lao Tzu, Alan Watts, and Krishnamurti, while also picking up popular self-help books of the day. He was open to all inspiration and all possibilities—his only limit being the limit of his own imagination and understanding.

I've come to develop a great fondness for experimentation in my own life. I run small tests and scenarios all the time to see what personal insights the results may bear. I've done everything from trying to say yes to all invitations for a certain amount of time to sitting with a particular chant for a specific number of days to drinking warm lemon water every morning. I've participated in rituals and workshops that appeal to me or followed my intuition fanatically for a period or decided consciously to engage in a particular relationship to see where it goes. And nowadays, during all these experiments, I try to hold the posture and stance of emptiness—nonjudgment and openness—so that I can try to really see, feel, and understand the optimal way of being for me.

Oftentimes it happens that I don't see an experiment through, and then there's information in that as well. Did I not stick to it because it wasn't working for me? Or did I stop because it was too hard or because I had some sort of blind spot or blockage that I ran up against? The possibilities for learning and growth are endless if you're prepared to dig in.

Most important, this position of experimentation makes everything a little less heavy and a little more fun. The new framework of curiosity and possibility can take the stress or fear out of the feeling that your decisions are monumentally fixed and finite. Set life up like an experiment, investigate and be open to the findings, and the heaviness of living may ease just a bit.

Put on Your Researcher's Hat

We did a program at the Bruce Lee Family Company that my friend and colleague Sharon Lee developed called Creative Fridays. One of the first assignments we were given was to go and participate in something that we were interested in or curious about but had never tried or experienced before. This meant we got to put on our researcher hats and go into the field as explorers.

I'm generally a little introverted by nature and sometimes find it challenging to enter social situations and converse comfortably, always relying on the hope that someone else will be a stellar conversationalist, and I can just hitch a ride. But when I was able to operate in the framework of researcher, I suddenly had a whole new perspective. I no longer had to be the nervous, conversationally challenged person with nothing to say. Instead I was on a mission of discovery. I could take the spotlight off me and put it squarely on the people I was researching.

With this newfound freedom, I said yes to all sorts of classes and social situations I had always been interested in but had never tried— breath work, parties where I didn't know anyone, Reiki. I was able to observe and converse with the others around me, and as a result I got to practice being a more open version of myself.

This stance of curiosity can be both freeing and engaging. Instead of being a passive participant, a bystander who waits to be called on or someone who puts all the pressure on themselves to be dazzling, you can give yourself the role of the adventure seeker, the detective, the journalist, or the anthropologist. When you become actively engaged, even just observationally, and look through the lens of curiosity, a whole new world will open up to you, and nothing will be as dull or as scary as you imagined.

This is the advice I'm always trying to give my teenage daughter when she tells me she's bored or that her teacher is lame. I tell her to challenge herself to see what she can discover and find interesting. Make it a game. See what there is to learn and observe about any situation. For instance, pause right now and take in your surroundings. Are you in a coffee shop? Are you at home in bed? How do you feel? Is this book engaging you? Do you feel energized and interested? Or is it a struggle to get through it and you're falling asleep? Are you in one of your happy places? Or are you distracted by noise and getting frustrated? What can you learn about yourself? Can you see what is frustrating you right now—this book, the noise, something that happened earlier today? What would you do differently? Or is this perfection? What can you learn about yourself right now that maybe you didn't already know?

There is always something to note. And sometimes the most valuable thing you discover is that what you're doing or where you are is not where you want to be—and that gives you the opportunity to begin charting a path out of there! That kind of information can be pure gold. It can save you from continuing to pursue a path that is leading you away from your soul.

Research Your Own Experience

One of the core mandates of jeet kune do and my father's life was this process: "Research your own experience. Reject what is useless. Accept what is useful. And add what is essentially your own."

As we saw in the opening story, it was extremely important that my father took full stock of his experience in that Oakland fight. Had he felt troubled by certain aspects of his victory but just casually pushed them aside until later (or until never, as is often the case), he would have missed a huge opportunity to grow and evolve. But because he took heed and gave serious attention to the entirety of his experience, in particular the troubling bits, he created a new art form and philosophy and went on to change the landscape of martial arts globally.

While Bruce Lee's life provides us with an impressive example, remember that we are focusing on *you* here, and the course and direction of *your* life. His life story is complete in the form of Bruce Lee. Yours is ongoing. And Bruce can be an amazing pointer of the way. In fact, he himself said:

> Remember, I am no teacher; I can merely be a signpost for a traveler who is lost. It is up to you to decide on the direction. All I can offer is an experience but never a conclusion, so even what I have said needs to be thoroughly examined by you. I might be able to help you to discover and examine your problem by awakening your awareness. A teacher, a good teacher that is, functions as a pointer to truth but not a giver of truth.

Another way to say this is: Don't give up your sovereignty or personal power. Claim your own path and your own experience. Be respectful and grateful for the signposts you encounter, the lessons you learn, and the teachers who point the way, but remember that you and you alone are responsible for your path and your growth.

As we discussed, there is always something to note about your experience. The best place to start is with how something makes you feel—energized or flat? Engaged or bored? This allows us to assess everything we experience with discernment and figure out what speaks to who we are. In this way, we are attempting to attain (or to remember) our nature. Recall that water stagnates and evaporates when it is not given what it needs to be itself—movement and connection to its source. In order for us to research our own experience, we need to be learning from what's around us—we need to be in full flowing connection to assess and pursue the energy that makes us feel most alive and good and essentially ourselves.

Understand Your Ignorance

The tricky part of researching our own experience is that we often don't understand our own ignorance. What is our own ignorance? It is a lack of understanding of our true selves—our soul, as it were. We do not understand what part we play in the creation of our lives so we point the finger outward rather than in. And that problem comes from ego. We frequently think we know what we want or what path we should be going down because our ego tells us what it thinks is best for us. Gary Zukav, in his book *The Seat of the Soul,* paints this as the struggle between the wants and needs of the personality versus those of the soul. So how do we tell the difference between what is of our ego, and what is of our soul or essence?

One key indicator that the ego is in the driver's seat rather than your soul is the word "should." If your decisions come from a place of "should" much of the time, then you're not necessarily being guided by your true, essential self. You may be giving up your authority to whomever the arbiters of "should" are—your parents, your partner, your teacher, your religion, society, etc.

Another time to watch out for the ego is whenever you find yourself overly interested in how you are perceived. The ego comes through in the image you have of yourself, and the attachment you have to being identified a specific way by others—i.e. your reputation. If you worry about what others think of you, if you need people to think you are a nice person, if you never want to be the bad guy, if you need to have the fancy house and car, then your ego is hard at work. Now, there's nothing wrong with having nice things or being a nice person, but does this drive how you act to the detriment of your peace of mind? Do you obsess over what others think and feel about you? Do you do things you don't really want to do because you need to be perceived a certain way? Is your self-worth dependent on external circumstances?

Once we've determined if we're operating from our ego self rather than our true self, how do we take it a step further to understand the cause of our own ignorance—especially if we are in fact ignorant of the source of the problem in the first place? Discovering our ignorance is actually a deep concept in Buddhist texts, looking at how we suffer because we place our happiness (or lack thereof) on attachments to things outside of ourselves. My father often spoke about this. Discovering our ignorance requires a lot of self-awareness and honesty, but it's possible to do so even if we are not yet totally self-aware. We just need to decide to really look. So where to begin?

One place you can start is with the "should"-ing. Listen to yourself and observe how you feel when someone presents you with a choice and you feel a "should" coming on. Your mom wants you to come for Thanksgiving. You have the thought you "should" go. How does that "should" make you feel? Alive? Or muted? If it makes you feel energized, then your "should" is actually an expression of your true self and therefore not a "should" but a recognition of something that is essential to you—family time, travel, etc. It is an expression of your heart. But if it makes you feel heavy or shut down (even just a little bit), that's something to take a look at. Why aren't you excited? Why does it feel heavy? Investigate! It may not change the decision, but it can illuminate the cause and help give you more clarity and more freedom. It can help you get to the bottom of what's of value to you and where you might need to do some work.

There are also clues in the word *ignorant* itself, which is rooted in the word *ignore*. What are you ignoring in your life? What thoughts keep nagging at you that you push away? What feelings come back again and again that you shove down and deny? What patterns keep playing out over and over in your life? I know a guy who is always telling me that people are bad-mouthing him and saying he's duplicitous. He tells me that it's not true; it's all gossip and rumors, and he doesn't know why everyone says these things about him all the time. Without a stance on what is true and not true, my suggestion to him is to ask himself the following: What is he doing or not doing that is making people feel ill at ease about his integrity? Then he can investigate with the intent to really look at himself and see what others might be seeing, and ultimately decide for himself if there are changes he needs to make.

Of course, some of the things that are actually good for you come with "shoulds" too, like "I should eat better" or "I should exercise more." These "shoulds" may be exactly what you need, but because you are "should"-ing them and/or pushing them away and ignoring them, they can feel heavy and therefore need to be examined. And perhaps it's not the eating or the exercising that's actually the issue, but your core wounds that are keeping you from showing up for yourself—wounds you continue to *ignore*.

Personally, I soothe with food and always have. Shifting that pattern has been a continuous struggle throughout my life. I probably vaguely recognized that I was doing it in my thirties. Then I berated myself for doing it for another decade but still had no way to change it. Food became a conduit for reward and punishment, for defiance and control, and for comfort and happiness, too. And you can't just stop eating altogether—food is necessary fuel!

Simply knowing it was happening wasn't leading me to a solution, in part because I wasn't actively trying to solve the problem in a curious and open way. I was acknowledging the existence of the problem but was too overwhelmed to do anything about it other than what was socially acceptable—complaining, being self-deprecating, following crazy diet and exercise fads, sometimes being a little overweight, sometimes feeling bad about myself, sometimes not. But I certainly wasn't looking for the cause of the issue. I'm not obese, I'd think, so how much of a problem is it really?

Well, if something is occupying a lot of your mental and physical energy, then it's a problem whether it's manifesting physically or not. And it's going to keep you locked into a life of ongoing inner struggle and personal negativity if you don't deal with it. After all, if you're honest with yourself, you already know what those things are that plague you internally, even if you don't know what to do about them.

Then one day in my early forties, I was recounting a memory to someone about my father's death. I was telling them about the visceral memories I had surrounding the Hong Kong funeral. It was a feeling of chaos. There were thousands of people lining the streets, large crews from every news outlet, fans crying on the sidewalks. It was an open-casket affair, and my mother, brother, and I were dressed in traditional white Chinese mourning garbs. We had to make our way in front of my father's body in full view of the TV cameras and photographers and do our bowing ritual before sitting on the ground in front of his coffin. I remember the chaos like a tornado swirling all around me, while I myself was shut down in the eye of the storm. I was numb and probably in a state of shock; after all, I was only four years old.

After the service, some kind human took me by the hand and said,

"Come on. Let's go get some candy." And I remember thinking, "Yes! Give me something that will make me feel some form of happiness right now that I can relate to."

And just like that, forty-something-year-old me had a revelation, mid-story, about one of the origins of my food issues. It is definitely not every piece of the puzzle, but it was enough of a connection for me to understand one cause of this lifelong issue. It had been there all along, but I hadn't connected to it because I wasn't really looking. I'd been hiding from the feeling of the death of my father and, in hiding from the feeling, I'd obfuscated a true look at this destructive pattern. My sense of safety had become wrapped up in a piece of candy (or a whole bag, knowing me), and I'd been operating under the hypothesis that my eating ineptitudes could only be controlled through strong denial of myself. [Pro tip: nothing is ever truly healed or resolved this way.]

I am on a path of understanding more and more about myself every day and shifting my perspective just like my father did. I'm becoming more conscious about what I'm ignoring or denying, and my learning process has become faster, my struggles fewer and less intense. This revelation about my self-soothing habits, while not the full solution, had given me something to explore, which led to an understanding of what else might need looking at. As my father himself said:

> Learning is discovery, the discovery of the cause of our ignorance; it is discovering what is there in us. When we discover, we are uncovering our own abilities, our own eyes, in order to find our potential, to see what is going on, to discover how to enlarge our lives, to find means at our disposal to help us cope and grow. Don't be in a hurry to "fix" things; rather, enrich your under-

standing in the ever-going process of discovery and find
more of the cause of your ignorance.

The Beginning of Really Seeing

My food breakthrough happened very haphazardly, but it doesn't have
to be so haphazard for you. Let this be a cautionary tale of how many
years of struggle can be avoided if you just proactively decide instead
to get conscious and start paying attention. Because, let's be honest,
if I wanted to know that information sooner, I could have chosen to
look more closely and see what was there. So I encourage you to open
yourself and look deeply, even when it's painful or scary.

I'm not going to lie to you: It takes courage to look at your issues,
it requires work to release them, and you may be frustrated at times.
You may feel as if you don't know what you're doing or what the next
best step is. It may shake you off what you thought was your foundation and make you feel a little insecure. You may decide it's just easier
not to look or know and just put up with the soul discomfort for the
rest of your life. But as you gain skill and practice, you will learn to develop ways to grow past that which scares you. And it will get easier—
and your process will actually become so intriguing to you that it will
start to engage your enthusiasm.

In the Oakland fight, my father was able to feel his struggle points,
his frustrations, and his fear, and rather than running from or burying
those, he said to himself, "Let's take a closer look." He believed that
"to understand your fear is the beginning of really seeing." You have
to be willing to look at the problematic pieces. If you won't look, and
look deeply, then you will never discover an important layer of yourself—a layer that may be holding you back or sabotaging you over and
over again and blocking your healing and growth.

Understanding your fear is a very important step in maximizing your potential. "Fear," my father explained, "compels us to cling to traditions and gurus. There can be no initiative if one has fear." He goes on to say that "the enemy of development is pain phobia—the unwillingness to do a tiny bit of suffering. As you feel unpleasant, you interrupt the continuum of awareness and you become phobic." The key then is to integrate these uncomfortable moments into your attention and awareness rather than turn away from them. And when you confront your fears, a miraculous thing happens: They lose their power over you. They become just another puzzle piece in the process of knowing yourself, another point of interest, another layer of discovery along the way.

Remember, don't beat yourself up over your fears or your shortcomings. We all have them, and they are just a road map for where you need to dig in and discover. And, as you are about to see, there's a flip side to what we consider our weaknesses.

Strengths and Weaknesses

Weaknesses and strengths are inextricably connected. You may think of them as separate—you have your weaknesses and then you have your strengths. Well, I've come to think of this duality of faults and assets as an IRL expression of yin yang. In looking more closely at myself, I've realized that I can't claim pride in my abilities without acknowledging their deficits as well and vice versa. For example, I'm very good at being alone. I like to be still and silent. I am strong and self-sufficient, and I'm not easily bored. And at the same time, I some-times isolate myself and then find it hard to connect with people. I don't ask for help when I could really use it. I'm good at muscling through life, but I can become drained and exhausted by this.

I've also discovered from many different experiences that I like variety. I like variety in what I eat, in my workday, and in things I do. I feel a kinship with spontaneity, surprises, and new experiences (even troubling ones). So naturally, and conversely, I struggle with routine. It took me until I was in my thirties to incorporate washing my face every night into my daily routine. I have a hard time paying bills on time and going through my mail regularly. I struggle with going to the grocery store and washing the dishes.

My strength of enjoying going with the flow and having new experiences makes handling the necessary, the routine, and the mundane hard for me. Discovering this about myself and realizing that my perceived "faults" were intimately tied to my strengths has helped me to keep perspective and maintain a sense of balance as I move through life. It also helps with not beating myself up, because every perceived weakness has a strength attached, and every strength, a weakness. So if I'm going to berate myself for my weaknesses, then I should be celebrating my strengths as well. Or we could just not make either thing good or bad and instead be with what is and keep moving forward (like water) toward the balance of flow we seek.

Self-knowledge is a game of balance—of understanding what we actually need in any given moment to flow through life. We need both rest and action. We need alone time and social time. We need self-reliance, and we need help. And we only come to understand in what way we need these things through investigating our true nature.

Ask yourself what you can discover about you. Start small. What can you learn about yourself from your favorite TV shows? What can you learn about how you want to be in the world from how you run your business or how you interact with your coworkers? What about from the challenging relationships you have and the conflicts you encounter? And what can this information tell you about the balance you need to strike between your strengths and weaknesses? What impulses do you need to control, and what controls do you need to loosen?

Maybe your favorite TV shows reveal that you love to laugh and see the romantic side of life, that you prefer beautiful ideals and joyous endings. But maybe this also reveals that you have a bit of an escapism practice. Maybe you struggle more with stressful, negative, real-life situations because they burst your bubble and really bring you down. Maybe you're actually a bit of a Negative Nellie in your real life because nothing is ever the way it is in the movies you like, or maybe you've set yourself up with an impossible bar to reach.

At work, maybe you are organized and pleasant with everyone. You treat everyone with a certain amount of respect no matter where they are on the business hierarchy. You always clean up your dishes in the workroom and you occasionally bring in treats for your coworkers. How lovely! Now check out the alternative. Do you get annoyed when others don't behave as you think they should? Do you in fact have an intolerance for messiness of any kind and judge people based on this? Have you developed a superiority complex with people because they aren't as "good" as you are? How are your relationships because of it? Are they great on the surface as you play the nice guy but not very deep? Do you feel like you can't just be yourself with all your warts and still be appreciated by everyone? Does the idea of being yourself mortify you?

Make a list. What are you good and bad at? Now, across from all the things on your list, try to write down what the strength and the weakness might be. For example, I am messy—but that also means I don't need everything to be perfect in order to function well (some people are paralyzed by mess). Spend a moment to see what you can notice about what you deem to be your strengths and your weaknesses. Can you see that they are trails of information that lead you to a clearer picture of yourself? Can you see how what you deem to be "good" and "bad" are in fact two sides of the same coin? And that when you own them in their entirety, it can help you create balance within yourself and release the notion of "good" and "bad" altogether?

> For it is easy to criticize and break down the spirit of others, but to know yourself takes maybe a lifetime. To take responsibility of one's actions, good and bad, is something else. After all, all knowledge simply means self-knowledge.

Self-Help

We are making these efforts to dive deeply into identifying, understanding, and working on our true selves because without that knowledge and practice, we cannot grow closer to our full potential and attain our natural, essential nature. We thus cannot become more like water. How we perceive ourselves and how we direct our thoughts is key to being able to flow. My father would say it's not *what* you think but *how* you think that's important. The "what" will become quickly influenced when the "how" is directed in the proper direction. Take this quote by way of example. It is one of my favorites from my father:

> We shall find the truth when we examine the problem. The problem is never apart from the answer; the problem is the answer.

Think about it concretely. When you look at a simple algebra problem like $3 + x = 10$, you cannot possibly solve for x without the other components. The answer is within the problem. It would be crazy for us to look at that math problem and start looking in the refrigerator for an answer. Yet this is what we do all day long. In particular, we do it by blaming others for our problems. That's not to say people don't stand in our way sometimes, but the solution is always in our own hands. Always. We just need to be more creative about how we look for the solutions that elude us.

Always late for work? Set your alarm clock ten minutes earlier. That's not the answer? Go to sleep earlier so you're not too tired in the morning. It's more serious than that? Take a look at whether or not you may be depressed. Oh, we're getting warmer? What is the root of your depression? Do you need to go seek help? Follow the problem. Try on some solutions, but follow the problem. See what you notice. Let the problem lead you.

My father would encourage us, as we sit with our problems, "to be alert, to question, to find out, to listen, to understand, and to be open." This is a great checklist for ourselves. Was I paying attention? Did I ask all the questions? Did I find out the answers? Was I listening? Do I understand what happened? Was I open to the whole experience? My father would caution us not to work for information but to "work for understanding," for "it's not how much you learn but how much you absorb in what you learn."

Bruce Lee wrote down his thoughts and actively processed his learning all the time. He didn't journal in the typical sense of the word, meaning he didn't have numerous bound journals that he neatly kept, but he did track his progress, write down his ideas, goal-set, dream, hypothesize out loud. He would craft letters and essays through numerous drafts. We'll discuss more of the ways in which my father used writing as a processing tool in chapter five. But from his own writings, we can see what was important to him, and what put him on the path to self-discovery—or, as he called it, self-help.

In one piece of writing from 1972, he noted that he had a deeply inquisitive nature and would ask himself these questions all the time as a youth:

What comes after victory?
Why do people value victory so much?
What is "glory"?
What kind of "victory" is "glorious"?

My father recalled how as a child he was a troublemaker and was greatly disapproved of by his elders. He says, "I was extremely mischievous, aggressive, hot-tempered, and fierce. Not only my opponents of more or less my age stayed out of my way, but even the adults gave in to my temper." He goes on to say he doesn't know why he was so truculent. Just that whenever he met someone he didn't like, his first thought was to challenge him. But challenge him with what? "The only concrete thing that I could think of was my fists," my father wrote. He continued, "I thought that victory meant beating down others, but I failed to realize that victory gained by way of force was not real victory." He recounts that later, when he became a student at the University of Washington, he was guided by a tutor to help choose his courses. The tutor, upon noting my father's inquisitive nature and his numerous questions, suggested he take some philosophy courses. The tutor told him, "Philosophy will tell you what man lives for."

My father noted that many of his friends and family were surprised that he was studying philosophy, since all he had ever been fanatical about was martial arts. They assumed he would go into some sort of physical education once in college. But my father quickly saw the connection between philosophy and martial arts. Recall that he wrote, "Every action should have its why and wherefore . . . I wish to infuse the spirit of philosophy into martial arts; therefore I insisted upon studying philosophy."

It was through the study of philosophy that he began to see the error of his former ways and to regret his previous assumptions about victory—but only because he could reflect honestly upon himself and his actions. Coming to the conclusion many years later, he realized, "Whether I like it or not, circumstances are thrust upon me and being a fighter at heart, I fight it in the beginning but soon realize what I need is not inner resistance and needless conflict, but rather, by joining forces, to readjust and make the best of it." Joining forces with the problems and the questions led my father to the solutions he was seeking and led him to a deeper understanding of his beloved martial arts and himself.

As you investigate and stick with the problem, I encourage you to utilize the tool of journaling or writing as a way of tracking your discoveries and organizing your thoughts. Don't just think your thoughts; write them down. Physically track what you love, what you're curious about, your experiments, your ideas, your dreams. If you just think them and don't truly represent them in a way that turns them into a concrete practice for you, then they may just float in on one wavelength and out on another, or exist only in a vague dream or recollection with no real plan of action.

Like when I first began running my company, I had an idea of what I was trying to accomplish, but I couldn't express it to anyone because I hadn't really taken the time to consider and work through what my vision, my mission, and my values were in concise, expressible terms. My employees could take directives from me and even trust me, but they were in the relative darkness about where the ship was headed because it just existed as a general thought in my own brain. This robbed all of us of some vital agency within our jobs.

Sometimes the act of funneling thoughts into physical form on paper can be a key part of self-actualizing and can give us the sense that our mental wanderings and discoveries are now being held accountable by us and will not be forgotten. The paper (or computer) can be a place to work through your process and list the questions that are pulling at you right now. It can be a work space, safety net, playground, or personal release. It can be a key to self-help.

In his work, my father set out clear guideposts along the path of discovery, and he advocated highly for self-help. Now, this doesn't mean that you need to live in the new age section of the bookstore (though he did advocate for prescriptive reading of all kinds of books; for him "specialized reading" was "mental food"). What he means by "self-help" is that you are the only one who can help yourself. Even in asking for someone else's help, you are helping yourself. Self-help, however you come by it—reading books, journaling, seeking a mentor, going to therapy, talking things out with trusted friends, meditating—is simply you sleuthing for your solution, looking for your discovery, learning what works or doesn't work, understanding your strengths and weaknesses. It is a process of self-empowerment.

As he said:

> I have come to discover through earnest personal experience and dedicated learning that ultimately the greatest help is self-help. There is no other help but self-help. Self-help comes in many forms: daily discoveries, honesty as we whole-heartedly do our best, indomitable dedication, and a realization that there is no end or limit because life is an ever-going process.

As we position ourselves to be curious, to look deeply at ourselves, we must be courageous in the face of our fears and ready to integrate our understanding into our experience. This state of constant independent inquiry that leads to new discoveries will be the means by which we uncover our potential and thus find our flow. Let it stand as a point of excitement and wonder that this learning, this uncovering, this process is limitless—and therefore, so is our potential.

> To be certain, every day there can be a revelation or a new discovery that I can obtain. I dare not say that I have reached any state of achievement, for I am still learning, for learning is boundless!

4

The Opponent

*To know oneself is to study oneself
in action with another person.*

Note: In this chapter, I will ask that we not approach the word *opponent* within the framework of an *adversary*. The idea of the opponent here is more along the lines of sparring partners—the people with whom we connect and who can ultimately challenge us, in beautiful and difficult ways, to be better versions of ourselves.

Lao's Time

In the movie *Enter the Dragon*, there's a scene we affectionately refer to as "Lao's Time." My father, as the character Lee, steps out of a meeting to instruct a student by the name of Lao. The young boy and my father bow to each other and the scene begins:

Lee: *Kick me. Kick me.*

Lao executes a very pretty side kick in Lee's general direction.

Lee stops him.

Lee: *What was that? An exhibition? We need emotional content. Try again.*

Lao executes another kick, but this time he grimaces a bit and throws an aggressive kick that is bigger and slightly unfocused. Lee stops him again.

Lee: *I said "emotional content." Not anger! Now try again. With me!*

Lao focuses in on Lee and throws a very concise kick directly to Lee's chest, followed by another one. The two move in harmony as Lao kicks and Lee moves with the kick. Lee is pleased.

Lee: *That's it! How did it feel to you?*

Lao: *Let me think. . . .*

Lee slaps Lao on the head as Lao turns away from the experience and gets into his head to try to analyze it. Lee admonishes him.

Lee: *Don't think! Feel. It is like a finger pointing away to the moon. Don't concentrate on the finger or you will miss all that heavenly glory! Do you understand?*

Lao nods at the advice. They square up to bow. Lao bows low, looking at the ground. Lee slaps him on the head again.

Lee: *Never take your eyes off your opponent, even when you bow.*

They bow eye to eye and the lesson ends.

This scene, which my father wrote to illustrate some of his thoughts on his philosophy of fighting, includes some of the most iconic lines from the film. It's a small exchange that holds so many juicy nuggets on his beliefs about martial arts, life, and relating authentically to "what is" in the moment.

Note that when the student first executes a perfectly lovely kick, my father says, "What was that? An exhibition?" In other words, who are you kicking? Why are you kicking? I mean, it's a pretty kick. It looks nice. But how does it relate to you and to me and to where we are in this moment? What is its purpose? What were you trying to express? The kick seems like a performance of a kick—disconnected from the circumstances.

"We need emotional content," he suggests.

The kid tries again, but he conflates the word *emotional* with the emotional context of attack. So he gets himself fired up and throws a wilder kick with an intense look on his face. But Lee admonishes, "I said 'emotional content'—not anger!" What my father means by emotional content is really context—being in current and appropriate relationship with the situation, feeling and sensing the energy of the present setting, i.e. what's happening in the moment. Anger would be the wrong context for this teacher–student situation. Lee continues: "Now try again—*with me.*" Be in relationship with me. Kick me. Direct your intent toward me. Come at me. I am here asking you to kick me with the correct intent for the context. So focus on me; give me your awareness; include me. In other words, actually try to do exactly what I've asked and kick *me.*

And so Lao tries again, and this time the kicks are focused; they have a target and a purpose. The two move back and forth, engaged in a symbiotic dance. Lee is ecstatic. Yes! That's it! And he asks Lao, "How did it feel to you?" Lao puts his finger to his chin pensively and turns away from Lee to contemplate. You see him literally turn away and go into his head to try to recapture and analyze the experience. Lee then raps him on the head.

"Don't think. Feel!" Don't separate yourself from the experience in order to analyze it. Don't isolate yourself from what just transpired. Don't disappear. Lee didn't ask, "What do you think?" He asked how it felt. What does it feel like to be engaged in this with me right now? Can you stay with me and with the sensation and respond directly to what's happening? He goes on to tell him, "It is like a finger pointing away to the moon; don't concentrate on the finger or you will miss all that heavenly glory!" Don't concentrate on only one part of the experience and miss the glory of the full experience, which is still unfolding and which is where the deeper understanding lies. And lastly he instructs, "Don't take your eyes off your opponent, even when you bow." Never fully disconnect and shut down even when it's time to leave. Stay present. Stay aware.

In the example above, the "opponent" relationship is a teacher–student one. The teacher (my father) is trying to get the student (Lao) to relate to him and the circumstance directly. He wants him to feel, to sense, to be in the moment with his sparring partner rather than just perform a well-executed but perfunctory lesson. He wants true engagement between them. After all, if a fighter is not in active relationship with his opponent, he will eventually be unprepared for what comes his way. In other words, he'll get popped. He'll be living a pattern behind a wall of isolation rather than living life. He'll be going through an order of operations or a program of moves rather than sensing the real-time changes in his partner and the setting and reacting accordingly.

What is combat, after all, but an intense relationship? Your opponent attempts to block and counter every strike you throw as well as land strikes of his own, which he will do in direct response to the signals he reads off you. He will also sense your energy, your reaction time, whether you seem confident or unsure, whether you move with experience, whether you hold his gaze, any patterns you have, etc. And while he is relating to you, he is adjusting himself as well. He is adjusting his strategy, his technique, his approach. If you land a strike, then he has to assess how you found an opening in him and vice versa. It's a dance. It's a relationship.

Does it sound familiar? It should, because we are assessing one another every day, sensing the energy and adjusting accordingly. You show up excited and upbeat for a lunch date with a friend, but when you arrive, you find them flat and morose. If you are aware, you probably downshift a bit. Maybe you ask what's wrong or you try to get them to laugh, but you respond to what you're getting based on what you're sensing. Even when we interact with a total stranger, like the checkout person in a store or the mailman, we notice if someone is rude or pleasant and we respond in turn with either an inward annoyance or a friendly smile. We are in relationship all the time, and our relationships are a reflection of our own inner world.

To learn and to grow, you need relationship. You need that sparring partner to level up your game. Simply put for our purposes here, there is no one better than the person standing before you at any given moment to help you see *yourself* more clearly. Someone who is there, whether they know it or not and whether you've known it or not, to show you where the pain points are, to show you how to be better and how to shine your light more brightly. Because you are in response to your environment all the time, your environment becomes a reflection of you. So what can you learn about yourself? Where can you discover the cause of your own ignorance? How can you become better from this? But be aware: You want to become better, not better than! The opponent relationship is not a contest.

The Non-Competition Model

This may sound strange, but Bruce Lee did not believe in competition. I mentioned earlier that he believed in fighting for real and that he didn't compete in the competitions of the day. But he came to the idea later in life that competition in general was not the correct model for personal or spiritual growth—or martial arts prowess, for that matter. To compete is to be bound up and focused on what is happening outside of yourself. Are you trying only to best someone else or win the prize? Or are you interested in your own process of growth? Competition categorizes everything and everyone into winners and losers rather than collaborators and cocreators. It separates us from self, and it pits us against one another.

Our potential can never be fully realized in competition because instead of thoroughly observing ourselves and maximizing the creation of our own experience, we focus on winning at all costs. We may spend hundreds of hours breaking down another's performance in order to best it while learning only very limited information about ourselves. And in this model, the information we do learn is grounded in what others have that we lack, rather than about what we possess that makes us who we truly are.

When we turn to water, we see a thing that is not in competition with its surroundings but in cocreation and coexistence with it. The water doesn't desire to best the earth. The water simply is. And the earth simply is. Sometimes the water overtakes the riverbank, and sometimes the riverbank changes the course of the water. In a state of neutrality or emptiness, because there is no comparison and no judgment, there is no competition. Life is not a competition; it's a cocreation. I often tell people that if you must compete, if that is a model that drives you (for now), then compete with yourself. Push yourself. Top yourself. Grow yourself. Inherent in competition is the

notion of winners and losers, but if we choose to approach each experience openly and neutrally and inhabit each moment fully, then
there's no room for winning or losing. There is only room for what
is unfolding before us and how we choose to respond. The sooner
we learn that there is no winning and losing in the big picture of life,
the sooner we can move from a sense of striving to the simple, active
state of being.

Sure, people win and lose at things all the time. And it can be argued there are external measures for whether or not a person lived a
"good" life. But only you will really ever know whether your life was
good for you. Only you know the level of satisfaction you have within
your heart and soul. Only you know what demons have plagued your
mental emotional space for years. So I suggest that, until the lights are
turned off for good on this life of ours, we work less on one-upping
each other and more on the lessons to be learned, the pivots we can
make, and the growth we can attain. Any winning and any losing is
only temporary. The stream doesn't do a victory dance and decide to
cease because it reached the ocean. It keeps on flowing.

At the end of the day, the person you should be keeping tabs on
is yourself. What is *your* experience of life and how can you make it
better wherever you find yourself? So when you are standing in front
of another person and you're all caught up in being better than or just
as good as they are, remember that all that comparison is a reflection
of the limited game you are playing.

> I'm not in this world to live up to your expectations
> and you're not in this world to live up to mine. . . . If
> you always put limit on everything you do, physical or
> anything else, it will spread into your work and into
> your life. There are no limits. There are only plateaus,
> and you must not stay there, you must go beyond them.

The Six Diseases

If we want to look at how we practice all forms of rivalry, there are six diseases my father wrote about, all of which stem from the desire we have to win at all costs. These diseases rely on being in competition, which is typically where we go in a relationship the moment any discord pops up. When we relate to others in these ways, we are disconnecting from them and disconnecting from our true selves in order to access some form of outside validation. In other words, there is no relationship, no collaboration, no cocreation. There is only the victor and the loser.

The Six Diseases are:

The desire for victory
I have to be the winner. If I don't win, I'm a loser. If I win, everyone else is a loser.

The desire to resort to technical cunning
I rely on the power of my wits to show you how great I am. Who cares about people or their feelings as long as everyone can see how clever I am?

The desire to display all that has been learned
Check me out. I know lots of things. I can speak at length about anything. It doesn't matter what anyone else has to say (especially if it's dumb).

The desire to awe the enemy
I am a force to be reckoned with. Look out! I will wow you to get your approval even if I have to do something shocking and wild to get your attention.

The desire to play the passive role
I am so easy to get along with. Who wouldn't like me? I am so unobtrusive and sweet. I will put anything that's important to me aside to make sure that you see how likeable and wonderful I am. How could you not like me when I sacrifice everything just for you?

The desire to rid oneself of whatever disease one is affected by
I am not okay as I am. I will perform constant self-work and read as many books as I can and take so many classes to make myself good that you will see that I am always trying to be a good person even if I continue to do lots of shitty things. I know I'm not okay as I am. And I know you know that I know I'm not okay as I am, which makes it okay not to get truly better as long as it looks like I'm trying.

With all of these pitfalls, there's an attachment to an outside outcome, which ultimately disconnects us from people and situations. There is only the desire to manipulate or shock and awe the "opponent." Even in the noble desire to be rid of the disease, there is a characterization of oneself as "the afflicted one" and therefore a denial of your own power.

I offer you these six diseases to consider as possible avenues of self-exploration because we have all participated in them when relating to another person or a situation. Can you recognize any of these in yourself? If you were to dig a little deeper, where would you find the wounding perception that motivates the disease and where could the healing begin? Allow yourself the awareness to notice your tactics and the freedom to feel your pain points. Realize that the diseases are just a delusion of the mind and the ego.

You complain about how judgmental people are? Guess what

you're being—judgmental. You give someone the cold shoulder for not being nicer to you? Guess what—you're not being nice. You gossip about what a gossip someone is? You're a gossip yourself. You get mad at someone for not loving you the "right" way—that's not very loving. Take a look in the mirror and see how you are extending the life of the disease rather than finding the cure and, ultimately, the healing.

These diseases are traps. They will keep you locked in isolation and stagnate your growth. They will keep your success always outside of yourself and out of your hands as you chase victory and validation through the eyes of someone else. And what's more, they will keep you from being fully yourself. Attachment to outcome is denial of one's true commitment to self.

> The great mistake is to anticipate the outcome of an engagement; you ought not to be thinking of whether it ends in victory or in defeat. See that there is no one to fight, only an illusion to see through.

The Sparring Partner

> Relationship is a process of self-revelation. Relationship is the mirror in which you discover yourself—to be is to be related.

Studying yourself in relationship is not about comparisons or judgments (i.e., competition). Think back to choiceless awareness and the empty mind. There is no right or wrong. There is only "what is." We don't need to shame ourselves or beat ourselves up in the process of making ourselves "better," nor should we shame and blame others to make ourselves feel better either. We need only observe, notice, and be curious about what is revealed through *our* responses and then choose how to move forward. Though simple in theory, this process isn't easy. To confront ourselves through the eyes of others can be sobering and uncomfortable, in particular if we aren't satisfied with where we are in life right now. But a relationship is also a clear reflecting pool in which we can see ourselves most astutely if we dare to really look.

When you pay my dear friend and intuitive counselor Tony Leroy a compliment, he responds by saying, "I'm just a reflection of you." It's lovely and, more important, it's true. After all, relating is an energy exchange between both parties. And we can choose to be conscious or unconscious about this. A relationship is the perfect place to practice learning and noticing ourselves. And not only relationships with partners, spouses, or close friends (though those are some key sparring partners), but relationships with everyone we come into contact with. We create our reality by how we choose to act and how we choose to respond to things outside ourselves from within ourselves.

So what makes a good sparring partner? Typically, when a fighter is getting ready for a bout, they want to spar with someone who will present a challenge, who can match or better yet slightly outmatch them blow for blow. If the fighter can too easily manipulate his opponent and knock them down, then they will not get to see for themselves what areas they need to work on. They will not be challenged to get better.

While there are the sparring partners we choose specifically to help us with certain things, we are actually encountering sparring partners everywhere. In particular, because there are aspects of our personalities that we are unaware of, we may not even realize who has good info for us as we move through life's journey. But if we get interested enough to notice our relationship dynamics and get curious about the exchanges we have and the other people involved in them, there are clues to figuring out the things we are hiding from ourselves.

Every encounter is an opportunity to understand our inner workings a little better.

Every time we point the finger away from ourselves, we should turn it right back around because the human across from us is in fact ourselves. I had someone I thought was a friend treat me like crap recently, and I was all up in my anger about it—complaining, seething, judging them for being incapable and unkind. But when I turned the finger around at myself, what I got to see was myself being judgmental and righteous. What I was really struggling with wasn't forgiving him for his unconscious (or even conscious) actions but coming face-to-face with my own. I couldn't forgive myself for having allowed myself to end up here. So every time I would get upset or reactivated over it, I would say to myself, "When I forgive him, I forgive myself." When I stopped judging him for his actions, I stopped judging myself for my reactions. I needed him to be wrong in order for me to be okay. And if that is what you need to be okay, well, is that really okay?

The Blame Game

> I have learned that being challenged means one thing and that is what is *your* reaction to it? How does it affect *you*? Now if you are secure within yourself, you treat it very, very lightly—just as today the rain is coming on strong, but tomorrow, baby, the sun is going to come out again.

Looking at our lives and ourselves in relation to others is important and valuable, but we need to be careful about what we think we notice or see. If you've ever seen a troubling reaction flash across someone's face while you were speaking or had someone snap at you for no reason or not call you when they said they would or ghost you, or, or, or . . . You know what happens. The stories and explanations start running through your head immediately in an effort to gather the evidence that supports your life theory. "She just doesn't like anyone." Or, "He is such a child!" We lose our empty mind, our neutrality, and jump right to the explanation for their behavior that makes us the hero or victim of the story. You assign all sorts of motives and blame onto others and make all kinds of justifications for yourself.

Your partner doesn't want to have sex with you tonight? Must be because he or she just doesn't like sex. Of course it has nothing to do with you. Or how you treat your partner. Or how emotionally absent you are from the relationship. Conversely, your friend didn't call you back after you texted her three times yesterday? She must not care about your friendship. Well, to hell with her!

The stories jump up strong and clear as soon as we sense a hurt. We attempt to rationalize, analyze, and explain them in ways that support our victimhood or our superiority. After all, it's easier to find fault with someone else than it is to acknowledge the wounds within ourselves. My father identified the motivation for this behavior this way:

> There is a powerful craving in most of us to see our-
> selves as instruments in the hands of others and thus
> free ourselves from the responsibility for actions, which
> are prompted by our own questionable impulses and
> inclinations.

So how do we not jump to create a narrative and deflect blame? How do we assess what is ours and what is another's? Well, first: Start from neutral. Empty that cup! Without making a story out of it, what actually happened? Next, open yourself up to the possibility that you may not know the full answer. Then, two words: *feel* and *speak*.

If you've taken up the mantle of the eternal student and know how to do the investigative work of getting to know yourself, then this process is easier because you already know what some of your stories and wounds are, what some of your weaknesses and strengths are. But if you aren't there yet, take a moment and feel deeply into your body. Does it feel like this is your issue or are you taking on someone else's? Or is it a little of both? How do you tell the difference? Try to be objective. Don't judge it or make it right or wrong. Discern. Stand a few feet back from it and ask yourself what part of this pattern or story sounds familiar to you. Listen to the language of your thoughts. Are you blaming? Or criticizing? Are you painting yourself as the hero of the story and the other person as the villain?

If you're still not sure, then open your mouth and speak. In the instance with your partner, ask him or her: Do you feel connected to me? Do you enjoy having sex with me? And with the friend: Is there something going on in your life that kept you from getting back to me? Is everything okay? Or make a request: I'd appreciate it if you could shoot me a quick text to let me know you got my message and you'll need to get back to me later. Two of Ruiz's Four Agreements are "don't make assumptions" and "don't take anything personally." Maybe you have been acting unappealingly and haven't been aware. Maybe your friend is having a bad day completely unrelated to you. How will you know what is happening if you don't allow yourself to fully connect and relate?

If you feel uncomfortable communicating directly and asking for what you want, notice that and investigate it. I saw a meme on the internet recently that intrigued me. It said: "Being scared to ask for what you need is a trauma response" (source unknown). Think about that. When in your life have you felt like your needs and wants were not valued? Why did you feel that way? Trace it back and untangle that knot.

Ultimately, we suffer because we put the responsibility for our happiness and our peacefulness outside of ourselves. We think we feel good or don't feel good because other people and events make us so. We form attachments to people, things, and happenings and assign them the quality of being attractive (I want this) or unappealing (I don't want this), and this gives them power over our inner world—our security, our confidence, our contentedness.

My father said, "Most [people] challenge [and blame] because they feel insecure and want to use a fight as a means to achieve some unknown aim." So take a moment to recognize that insecurity and then get to know what the aim within your heart is. Search out the wounds. Are you blaming someone else for something that's present in yourself? Are you offering people the benefit of the doubt around their reactions and seeking to find out what's really going on with them, or just coming in for the attack or the brush off? Watch and learn from what you project in the mirror of relationship. Everything we need to know is there for us if we have the courage to get in the ring and spar.

Own Your Sh*t

Accepting that the man in the mirror of relationship is always ultimately you and relinquishing the blame game means owning your own shit. That requires being honest with yourself about how you show up in the world—what you allow, what you accept, and what you proliferate.

A while back I was in an on-and-off relationship that went on for a number of years, and I always felt undervalued and dissatisfied, yet I kept going back. He would tell me how much he loved me and make all kinds of promises about things we would do, ways we would be, places we would go. The words were phenomenal. So when the actions wouldn't follow, I was often confused. He wouldn't say he wanted to do all these things with me if it weren't true, right? He says he loves me, so it must be that he just doesn't know *how* to love me! So I need to show him by being super loving and giving to him . . . right? And then he'll get it.

I had this idea in my head that if I could model the care I wanted (without having to actually ask for it) and by example have him adopt it, then that would thereby prove my worth. It felt like if I could just make this man care for me the way I wished to be cared for without having to demand it, it would somehow validate my specialness. I was looking for someone else to validate me rather than supporting and validating myself. Sound familiar?

What happened instead is perhaps not surprising: this person continued not to care for me or show up for me despite what he would say, and I would break it off again and again. I finally ended it for good after a particularly bad spell of stonewalling and being misled, and I then blamed him for undervaluing and dismissing me. Framing it this way meant I got to be righteous and hurt. But who was really doing the undervaluing and the blaming? Who was putting on the grand performance of care or not care? In order to truly heal and move past this pattern, I had to take responsibility for what I had allowed, and how I had failed to show up for myself. As it turns out, I had been the one who hadn't valued me. I hadn't been caring for myself. He was just reflecting me back to me. That's not to say his behavior was okay, but it didn't absolve me either.

What followed was some of the deepest personal work I have done. After a lot of anger and disappointment (all of which, while understandable, was not useful in helping me heal or grow), I had to look deeply at myself and acknowledge how I had let myself down, and how this relationship had sprung out of my own personal wounds and issues. That was a hard realization to come to, but it led to a deeper sense of self-love, self-worth, gratitude, and lessons finally learned that won't need to be repeated in another relationship. Since taking personal responsibility and healing this area of my psyche, I began to experience more personal peace and contentedness than I have ever known up to that point. I have never felt so whole.

But I wouldn't have been able to get there if I'd just continued to play the blame game and acted like my shit didn't stink. And there was a lot of blame to play—so I did just that for a solid while, believe me. But the truth of the matter is that this was a pattern I had been repeating in all my relationships up to this point. This was simply a different flavor of the same thing. I had gotten out of other relationships that weren't working, but I hadn't learned the lesson of those relationships because I had refused to look very deeply in the mirror at the real culprit—me. I wasn't owning my shit. After yet another go-around in this particular relationship pattern, it was time to ask myself why this was really happening, to look deeply at my fears and my hurts, and to finally accept myself, forgive myself, and level up.

We often get stuck in self-criticism and righteousness over our mistakes and our shortcomings, but as I said above, doing that does not create healing or a sense of inner peace. There's nothing wrong with mistakes or failings or harsh realities. In fact, sometimes we need them to get truly real with ourselves. As I discovered from this experience, it was time to take a good hard look past the self-righteous, ego-based image of myself and into my heart and soul and see what was actually inside me. It was time to feel into my relationships with more sensitivity in order to get a better picture of my relationship with myself.

> It is not a shame to be knocked down by other people. The important thing is to ask when being knocked down, "Why am I being knocked down?" If a person can reflect in this way, then there is hope for that person.

True Communication, True Relationship

Even as my father was creating the art of jeet kune do, he continued to always practice a basic wing chun exercise called chi sao, which translates to "sticking hands." In this type of sensitivity training, two practitioners maintain contact with each other's forearms while they execute techniques. They tune into changes in pressure and momentum with great sensitivity in order to be able to feel when there is an opportunity to attack and when they need to counter an opponent's movements precisely, quickly, and with appropriate response. This exercise is often practiced blindfolded so that you have to hone in very directly to the sensation of your opponent and his movements. The drill claims to cultivate lightning-quick reactions and the ability to almost read your opponent's mind.

In chi sao, the practitioners rock their arms side to side in a circular motion, never releasing the tension on their forearms and never stopping the motion. They continue to exchange energy back and forth, all the while sensing what the other is giving and then trying to respond skillfully and immediately. This is a truly connected relationship in which both sides are in full communication, contact,

and sensitivity to each other, and in which both sides are pushing the other onward. This exercise requires great attention and presence, but it is also meant to prepare you to find the opening through which you will act.

So how will we act when we encounter a challenging person or situation? Do we just skirt around and avoid it or them altogether? Maybe. When it's someone or something that we aren't that invested in, then yes; maybe that's fine. But what if this is one of our deepest relationships and it hits on one of our deepest wounds? What if the opposition we are meeting is within a very close relationship of ours where the stakes are emotionally high and we don't want to just walk away? As my father wrote:

> Instead of opposing force by force, one should complete an opposing movement by accepting the flow of energy from it and defeat it by borrowing from it. This is the law of adaptation.

In martial arts, this "law" could be akin to the idea of using the movement of someone's strike to create an opening for your own action. Like in the chi sao exercise, this means being so attuned to your opponent's energy that you can sense the opportunity to respond immediately. In a challenging personal situation, you can borrow the energy a person or situation is giving you and adapt that to the appropriate response. I say "appropriate response" here because unlike in a fight, we are not looking for the opening in which we can strike at the other person. The opening we are looking for is the one where we get to respond sincerely and with proper intent toward the meaningfulness of this particular sparring partner. Ultimately, we are also looking to stay open enough to learn something important about our sparring partner, ourselves, or the situation.

Let's take the example of the guy I was seeing who was saying all the right things but not holding space for our relationship. In the beginning, I opposed that with force—I got mad. I tried to get him to take notice of me by first demanding his attention in petty ways and then flinging my hurt at him. All that did was make him pull away and put up more resistance, because who wants to be in a relationship with a petty and angry person? I was meeting his wall with my full-scale assault (force meets force). Instead I ultimately did the right thing and accepted the situation by borrowing from him what he was giving me (force adopts force), and I turned away. Thus, the water flows along the barrier and onto greater depths. It was the better and more powerful move because it preserved my dignity and my energy, bolstered my sense of self, and led me away from an impossible situation. I was taking care of myself rather than trying to get someone else to do it for me. And so I completed our relationship with the energy he was giving to it—the energy of withdrawal.

This was only possible by accepting what I was being shown through the mirror of our relationship. And the lessons I went on to learn about myself were only possible by looking honestly and deeply at what I had brought to this relationship. I transformed and healed myself, not through avoidance but rather by directly relating to and borrowing from the situation and meeting myself there in the process.

I love the quote below because it speaks to the depth of how much we are reflected in the things we encounter throughout our experience. We encounter the world every day, all day, and if we know how to look at it, if we can listen to our inner stories and how we are reacting to everything, then we will find that what we encounter is our love, our pain, our healing, our likes and dislikes, our beliefs, and more. We will find that what we encounter is ourselves.

The world and I are both in active correlation. I am that which sees the world, and the world is that which is seen by me. If there were no things to be seen, thoughts to be imagined, I would not see, think, or imagine. I acquire no understanding of myself except as I take account of objects, of the surroundings. I do not think unless I think of "things"—and there I find myself.

There Is No Me

To live is a constant process of relating; so come on out of that shell of isolation and conclusion and relate directly to what is being said. Do not make up your mind as to "this is this" or "that is that." Begin to learn to investigate everything for yourself from now on. The oneness of life is a truth that can be fully realized only when a false notion of a separate self—whose destiny you consider apart from the whole—is forever annihilated.

We have used the word *opponent* throughout this chapter in talking about that which we relate to, but what is really meant is a symbiotic relationship between me and what I perceive as outside of me. And "outside of me," we are discovering, is actually also me, because the world and I are always in active correlation—so there is no "outside of me." Rather, like the principal of yin yang, there are no actual opposites but instead only complements. "When we hold to the core, the opposite sides are the same as if seen from the center of a moving circle." My father also put it another way—"To change with change is the changeless state." In other words, when I express my true self and move with the world rather than against it, then change becomes something to flow with rather than resist.

In looking at our "opponents," we must not be afraid to uncover our true self and let that be seen. And in being comfortable enough in our own skin to be vulnerable and real, we suddenly begin allowing others the comfort of their true identities as well. If we do the work of understanding who we are, we will hold more and more to our core and see the opposing points of view more as complements rather than condemnations. Remember, opposites isolate us and create false distance. In reality, there is no distance—everything is connected like one fluid motion of a wave.

Remember the last part of my father's water origin story when he was out on the boat? A bird flew by and cast its reflection on the water, and in that moment, he realized that when he was facing an opponent, what he needed to do was feel his feelings and think his thoughts, and then allow them to pass through like a reflection rather than get hung up on them. He said, "Should not the thoughts and emotions I had when in front of an opponent pass like the reflection of the bird flying over the water? . . . not being without emotion or feeling, but being one in whom feeling was not sticky and blocked."

Wouldn't that be nice? To be able to have your feelings and thoughts and allow others to have their feelings and thoughts? And to be able to share your feelings and thoughts without having to make a case for yourself or against someone else? You just come together, share, and then walk away, both intact—maybe having opened each other's eyes to something new. And if the relationship is toxic in some way, you can always walk away intact and still allow them to keep what's theirs at a safe distance.

So take a moment to consider with me the possibility of holding relationship to others in this way: Picture a full, bright moon shining down on a pool of still water. On one side is the water and on the other is the moon. As they hold and reflect each other, notice that each makes the other even more resplendent.

> As the water manifests the brightness of the moon, the
> moon manifests the clarity of the water.

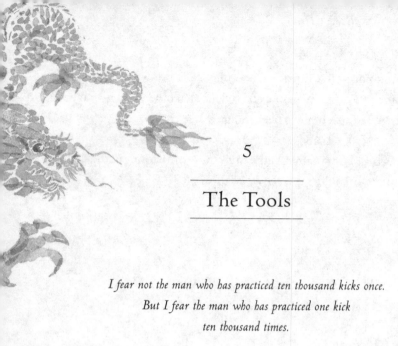

5

The Tools

I fear not the man who has practiced ten thousand kicks once.
But I fear the man who has practiced one kick
ten thousand times.

What's Your Kung Fu?

In this chapter, we'll start to get more prescriptive. What are some concrete tools we can use to embody and integrate the principles we're learning? How do we translate concepts into true skills? The simple answer is: consistent practice. I wish I could tell you there's a magic spell that would just make you be like water. But as the quote above indicates, we need to practice one kick ten thousand times until it becomes second nature. First, however, let's identify our own kung fu.

The literal translation of kung fu is skill achieved through hard work and discipline. The exact translation itself has no ties to martial arts, though it has become associated with Chinese martial arts over the centuries, given the amount of hard work and discipline it requires to become a master. That said, it is possible to have good kung fu in anything: mathematics kung fu, mothering kung fu, public speaking kung fu. You get the point. It is also possible to have life kung fu or *you* kung fu. One simply need put in the practice. So, what's your kung fu, or what do you want it to be?

If you are interested in trying to cultivate your potential, self-actualization, and flow, then there is part of you that believes in and senses the energy of your spirit (your aliveness) that resides within your body, and the possibilities it holds for you. You wouldn't be reading this book if that drive weren't already in you somewhere. There is part of you that is wanting something more for your life. There is part of you that dreams a dream of being fully alive and joyous and impactful in a positive way, no matter how much fear or doubt you have.

No matter what your personal kung fu is, this chapter will present a series of tools and exercises that can get you out of your own way and highlight your path forward. They will help you systematically expand your energy from idea to execution so that you can create the alive and centered version of yourself that you always knew was hiding just below the surface. And as Bruce Lee has shown us, the first step toward growth is action.

Can't Stop, Won't Stop

On March 27, 1968, my father did 500 punches with his right hand followed by 250 punches with his left. He then did a series of ab exercises—7 sets each of leg raises, sit-ups, and side bends. He later did some supplemental punch training—another 500 punches with his right hand and 250 with his left. He then cycled 2 miles (in 7 minutes), followed by one more set of 500 punches with his right hand. He followed this up by training with Ted, Herb, and someone named Dave at 7:30 P.M. And the day before that was similar—throwing in a 1-mile run with my mom as well. How do I know this? He tracked it in his daily planner.

Bruce Lee charted his progress. He set goals. He created reminders and exercises and tools for his growth—physically, mentally, and spiritually. If he didn't have a specific tool, he created it (or had someone create it for him). If he was unsure about what would work, he experimented and tracked the results until he could find the best way forward. He was a creator and an inventor, part artist and part scientist—truly a renaissance man.

When my father first started adding cross-training exercises to his martial arts routine, he got into weight lifting. He had a good friend named Allen Joe, who was a professional bodybuilder. So he went to

Allen and asked him to show him some exercises. He started imple-
menting these techniques, and he got results. But what he noticed was
that while he was getting stronger, he was getting bulky bodybuilder
muscles because of the types of exercise he was doing, and those
were slowing him down in his martial arts techniques. He didn't scrap
weight lifting altogether, however. Rather, he made adjustments. He
could see the benefits of the weights; he just had to incorporate them
into his routine in a way that served his ultimate purpose and worked
for him specifically. So he started to play around with lighter weights
at higher reps and then moved on to isometric training (bringing the
muscle to failure as quickly as possible) until he had a routine that
yielded the results he was looking for—a strong, lean body that could
react instantly.

But let's get one thing straight. Bruce Lee was not promised or
fated to become phenomenal. Yes, he was extremely physically coor-
dinated and innately driven. But he was also terribly nearsighted, of
average height (five foot seven inches), and sickly and thin as a kid.
One of his legs was slightly shorter than the other and he was rejected
from the military for his eyesight and certain other physical defects
they deemed limiting. And as a young man, he had a temper that got
him expelled from one school and almost landed him in gangs and jail
and worse.

Bruce Lee was phenomenal because he worked relentlessly to be
phenomenal. Yes, he had some great raw ingredients, but without the
hard work, there would have been no global icon. And we all have
some great raw ingredients too. I remind you of this because sometimes people think that Bruce Lee was just talented, i.e., extraordinary in a way that they are not. Well, if that's true, then one of his
extraordinary talents was his work ethic and his attitude. And that, my
friends, can be cultivated!

I have heard story after story about how my father was always training, stretching, writing, reading, teaching, working, so I had to ask my mom if he ever just did nothing. And (to my personally selfish dismay) she said, "No." Even when he was reading a book or watching a boxing match on TV, he was also stretching or doing something active. He would take the stairs instead of the elevator, and if he had to wait for an elevator, he would drop and do push-ups while he waited. Yep—that's my dad!

You can say he was driven or passionate or obsessed, or maybe he had a sense of his internal clock and knew he had limited time. Call it what you will, but he had an inner fire that he felt and, more important, gave his attention to. And not only did he heed this fire, but he fanned its flames by creating practical methods by which to encourage its growth and intensity. He wasn't going to be stopped by lack of imagination or lack of effort in the pursuit of the realization of his potential and his dreams. "Knowing is not enough," he said. "We must apply. Willing is not enough, we must do."

So yes, if Bruce Lee was born superhuman, then it was his superhuman drive that exceeded that of mere mortals. And though you may think you can't cultivate drive, you're wrong. You absolutely can. But it will take effort; it will take consistent practice. As mentioned, this chapter features some of the tools he used to train himself, body and soul. By taking a look at these tools, you will get to see his process and figure out for yourself if any of the same systematic approaches he took can help you cultivate yourself and your drive.

What follows is by no means an exhaustive list. And the tools discussed in this chapter are meant to be utilitarian; the big existential stuff comes later. The one thing you really need to know is this: these tools will not work if the intention for transformation and the commitment to finding your way are not there. So take them or leave them, but the path is yours to walk.

Tool #1—Take Aim

In 1969, my father created a document entitled "My Definite Chief Aim." It was a single piece of paper written in his handwriting that stated:

> I, Bruce Lee, will be the first highest paid Oriental super star in the United States. In return, I will give the most exciting performances and render the best of quality in the capacity of an actor. Starting 1970 I will achieve world fame and from then onward till the end of 1980 I will have in my possession $10,000,000. I will live the way I please and achieve inner harmony and happiness.

The document is signed by him and dated January 1969. This is some serious goal-setting. Of course, he died before he was able to attain the ten million dollars, and it was more like 1973 when he achieved world fame, though it can be argued that he started working toward that with great result in 1970, which is when he did his first film in Hong Kong. All told, I'd say he did a pretty good job in the few years he had.

So do you have a *big* goal or dream? It's okay if you don't. You don't have to. I don't. Not really. If I do, it's something totally nebulous and grandiose like "change the world for the better." I have lots of little concrete goals that maybe one day will amass into one big, definitive one. But if you do have a big goal or dream, write it down clearly and energize it.

What do I mean by energize it? In books about "the law of attraction" like *The Secret,* you hear over and over that you have to believe in your goal like it's happening right now. But that can be hard to do, because as practical humans, there's part of us that may not believe that and may struggle with the logic of it, and then the law of attraction doesn't seem to work. Rather, I would suggest that you energize your goal by letting it re-excite you every time you think about it. This goal should rev you up. It should make your heart beat a little faster or make your imagination soar. So every time you come back to it, reengage with that feeling of enthusiasm for it. Rejoice in the dream. And then use that ignited feeling to energize you along the path that will get you there. In other words, live into the possibility and the feeling of the ultimate goal.

A big goal like this should feel very clear to you. If the goal is not clear, it will be hard to work toward and therefore hard to achieve. Don't get stuck in the exact "how" of your goal, meaning the exact steps you will take to get there; that may not unfold the way you expect it to. It may morph and change along the way—so rather than getting caught up in the exactitude of "how," stay with the clarity and the energy of your ultimate vision and be open to the possibility that your path may take some unseen twists and turns as the journey unfolds. Though the goal may evolve a bit, the clarity and the energy of it should remain.

Even before my father had written down his definite chief aim, he had already established a lot of clarity around what he wanted to accomplish. In 1962, at the age of twenty-one, he wrote a long and insightful letter to a family friend in Hong Kong named Pearl Tso. After spending a few years in the United States, my father noticed that Japanese arts such as karate and judo were fairly prevalent in the United States, but not Chinese kung fu. Recognizing a wide-open opportunity to share the art and culture he loved, my father laid out a vision for the trajectory of his life as a kung fu teacher in this letter to Pearl.

> My aim is to establish a first Gung Fu Institute that will later spread all over the U.S. (I have set a time limit of 10 to 15 years to complete the whole project). My reason in doing this is not the sole objective of making money. The motives are many and among them are: I like to let the world know about the greatness of this Chinese art; I enjoy teaching and helping people; I like to have a well-to-do home for my family; I like to originate something; and the last but yet one of the most important is because gung fu is part of myself.
> . . . Right now, I can project my thoughts into the future. I can see ahead of me. I dream (remember that practical dreamers never quit). I may now own nothing but a little place down in a basement, but once my imagination has got up a full head of steam, I can see painted on a canvas of my mind a picture of a fine, big five or six story Gung Fu Institute with branches all over the States. I am

not easily discouraged, readily visualize myself as overcoming obstacles, winning out over setbacks, achieving
"impossible" objectives.

Can we pause a minute to admire his crystalline clarity? He says
what he wants to do and why he wants to do it, he says what about
this resonates and feeds his soul, and he sets a clear timeline for his
goals while acknowledging the difficulty of the path ahead. Beautiful.
And clear.

Clarity of purpose is important not only because it helps us to
move decisively forward with a plan of action, but because when the
obstacles come (and they will come), you will need the intensity and
clarity of your soul's purpose to keep you from getting lost in the
difficulties you encounter or derailed by the well-intentioned people
around you who see things differently than you do along the way.
Clarity helps you continue to take aim.

If you do the work to really know yourself, that intimate knowledge of who you are will help you to remain grounded and (as my
father liked to say) "function from your root." And cultivating this
clear center will produce in you the feeling of security, assuredness, and assertiveness—in particular when the going gets rough
or when you decide it is time to change things up or go to the next
level. Knowing who you are, what you want, and what you love
will serve you faithfully. And then, having clear objectives and clear
dreams will set a direct trajectory from which you will not easily
be deterred.

Being clear can sometimes be half the battle. If you can't feel the
dream in your heart and see it in your mind's eye, then it may not be
your dream. It may be someone else's. Your dream should excite and
entice you. It should make all the hard work and potential struggle
you are going to have to put into it worth it, because it is all yours.

Tool #2: Take Action

My father had a poster that he kept hanging on the wall of his office. Years later, after he passed, this same poster hung on the wall of my brother's bedroom as a teen, and now it hangs on the wall in my office, and it makes me smile every time I see it. This poster is a very 1970s, almost-black-light-looking thing that shows two cartoon vultures sitting on the branch of a dead tree overlooking a barren desert landscape. There is a cow skull on the ground and no living thing for miles. In the poster, one vulture is turning to the other one and saying, "Patience, my ass! I'm gonna kill something!"

This poster is *so* my dad. Although he believed in patience and gentleness and the ability to yield, as we'll get to soon, he was also not one to tread water or waste time. He was going to do all he could do to move in the direction of his unfolding, and if that meant taking some extra measures, well, then that's what he was going to do. If whatever action he took didn't work out, then he wouldn't spend very long banging his head against a wall or continuing to push for something that wasn't working. In his mind, why wait for something that may never come if you may be able to manifest it yourself? And how will you know if you could have manifested it yourself if you never even try?

What was remarkable about Bruce Lee was just how much of a man of action he truly was. That doesn't mean he didn't dream. In fact, he dreamed big and then worked his ass off. One mantra of his was, "Be a practical dreamer backed by action." And let's not get hung up on the word *practical*. *Practical* here means you believe that the dream is possible. For Bruce Lee, being an authentic and powerful Chinese leading man in 1970s prejudiced Hollywood was a practical dream.

When we have dreams and goals that we don't follow through on, we stagnate. Our brains, however, never cease thinking and our bodies never cease feeling, and so we get full up on thoughts and feelings that we aren't doing anything about—and then enter action paralysis. And because we are in action paralysis, we begin to acquire mounds of evidence that we aren't capable or deserving of those dreams, and so we start to let go of the dreams. Whereas, when we act, even in a small way, by writing a goal down on paper and taking the first step, for instance, we begin to build energy toward our goals. Action begets more action. Even the laws of inertia back this up. Remember Newton? "An object at rest stays at rest and an object in motion stays in motion." Be the object in motion.

Once we know we want to pursue a goal or cultivate a practice, we must give ourselves over to the actions we choose to take. How do we do that? We can start by getting clear about what it is we want to do, per the first tool. Take aim. And if we aren't totally clear about the big places we want to go, then we can start by taking smaller actions (aka baby steps) toward the little things we know we want in order to ultimately get clear about the big picture. You want to do something major with your life but you can't even seem to keep your apartment clean? Then start by cleaning your apartment. Then what else is blocking your path? Go there next. No matter how silly or unrelated it may seem, handle the stuff that is bothering you. Build your confidence up so that you can take care of your business and solve your own problems. Sometimes my day feels like a total success if I manage to make it to the grocery store.

So we begin. We practice. We experiment. We try things—and with the proper attitude. Attitude is everything. My father said, "If you think a thing is impossible, you'll make it impossible. Pessimism blunts the tools you need to succeed." A bad attitude slows you down and hinders your ability to succeed.

You can always alter your path of action as you try things and receive the results of your experiments. After all, staying present on the journey means we're aware enough to know when a certain direction isn't working. But if we are not present and aware *and* we have a negative attitude, then we will remain confused and scattered along the way. When we don't act in clarity and when we don't stay present, we don't reap the benefits of strength and confidence that we should get from the actions we are choosing to take.

Sometimes the hardest part of taking action is making the first move. Thinking about doing something isn't the same as actually doing it. It takes some willpower to get up off the couch, and sometimes the action paralysis is so great that you just can't seem to make yourself go to the gym no matter how badly you want to get in shape. We will talk more about willpower soon, but let's consider that what may be holding us back is our attachment to the results and what they mean about us if we don't achieve them. It seems easier perhaps not to try rather than try and fail. There's no shame in failure if you never tried in the first place, right? Unfortunately, you still have to live with yourself and inside yourself, and that stuck place can feel terrible. So instead let's talk about a couple of things to help motivate us to take action toward the dreams in our hearts. As my father said, "In great attempts it is glorious even to fail."

In the first tool of this chapter, we talked about staying tapped into the energy of the big goal and letting it reignite you whenever you get stuck. That proves helpful when it comes to igniting action. And in chapter two, we talked about emptying your cup and staying neutral. If there's no right and wrong or judgment over this and that, then there's no need to beat yourself up because there's no win or lose. When you notice you didn't do what you wanted to do, then just give yourself a little pep talk and start again as if the past is, well, past. Every moment is a new moment to pick it back up and start again. Remember that practice doesn't make us perfect; it makes us *better*. So stop attaching yourself to the results and just stay committed to the path. And when you stumble, pick yourself up and begin again.

"Action is a high road to self-confidence," my father said. Take one small action, and let that action lead to confidence, and let the confidence create energy toward more action—and from snowmelt, a surging river will form.

Tool #3—Affirm

You've probably heard of affirmations—positive sayings you repeat every day that you want to ingrain for yourself. My father used affirmations as part of his practice. Among his writings were seven affirmations that worked as an ecosystem of the mental/emotional state that he wanted to cultivate for himself as he moved through his day. He would carry them around with him in his appointment book or on laminated note cards and pull them out from time to time so he could refer to them throughout the day.

These are his seven affirmations:

Memory
Recognizing the value of an alert mind and an alert memory, I will encourage mine to become alert by taking care to impress it clearly with all thoughts I wish to recall and by associating those thoughts with related subjects which I may call to mind frequently.

Subconscious Mind
Reorganizing the influence of my subconscious mind over my power of will, I shall take care to submit to it a clear and definite picture of my major purpose in life and all minor purposes leading to my major purpose, and I shall keep this picture constantly before my subconscious mind by repeating it daily!

Imagination
Recognizing the need for sound plans and ideas for the attainment of my desires, I will develop my imagination by calling upon it daily for help in the formation of my plans.

Emotion
Realizing that my emotions are both positive and negative, I will form daily habits which will encourage the development of the positive emotions and aid me in converting the negative emotions into some form of useful action.

Reason

Recognizing that my positive and negative emotions may be dangerous if they are not guided to desirable ends, I will submit all my desires, aims, and purposes to my faculty of reason, and I will be guided by it in giving expression to these.

Conscience

Recognizing that my emotions often err in their over-enthusiasm, and my faculty of reason often is without the warmth of feeling that is necessary to enable me to combine justice with mercy in my judgments, I will encourage my conscience to guide me as to what is right and wrong, but I will never set aside the verdicts it renders, no matter what may be the cost of carrying them out.

Willpower

The power of will is the supreme court over all other departments of my mind. I will exercise it daily when I need the urge to action for any purpose, and I will form habits designed to bring the power of my will into action at least once daily.

Yes, Bruce Lee, the seemingly most confident man in the world, worked on his mental and emotional state directly and purposefully. Maybe that's why he was so confident? He exercised not just his body but his will and his emotions and all the facets of his mind, too. He believed wholeheartedly in the power of autosuggestion and positive framing. He believed that optimism was a kind of faith that one needed to deliberately practice and cultivate within themselves.

Sometimes people struggle with affirmations. Affirmations can feel kind of cheesy or unrealistic, or like you are lying to yourself because you are saying things about yourself that you suspect aren't true, no matter how much you want them to be. But the most effective element of affirmations (and dare I say most things) is the perspective you hold in the execution of them. Instead of doubting the affirmations because they aren't true right now, try framing them a different way: that they just aren't true *yet*.

With an affirmation, you are trying to plant seeds in your subconscious or unconscious mind that will take root and grow into your consciousness as you continually affirm them over and over. After all, your subconscious mind is really the driver of your personality and your actions, so we want to suggest to it that it should grow some new ideas to orient you in a better direction.

I trained in kickboxing with Sensei Benny "the Jet" Urquidez, a competitive full-contact kickboxing fighter who was undefeated in his career and held six world titles in varying weight classes (to name only one aspect of his many accomplishments as a human). When we would train, he would ask me to execute some kick or some move, and I would try it and blow it, and then I would say, "I can't do it." And he would freeze and look at me with his piercing eyes and say, "Yet! You can't do it yet." And he would say this over and over and over again to every complaint and frustration I would spew. It was positive framing and it was firm. If you just keep practicing, then one day you'll get it.

Another way to access the power of your affirmations is to write them down in a way that frames them as something you are in the process of, so that they feel more possible and more aligned with where you are right now. So instead of "I am strong and fit," you could write, "I am working every day to be strong and fit." This way you can still affirm what you want and feel authentically connected to it.

Give it a real try, and see if it works for you. Do it every day for a month. Start to notice if the thoughts you want to affirm begin to pop into your mind unprompted and frequently. Notice if the affirmations are helping you modify any behavior you are trying to change or the way you feel throughout the day or your view on life. Do you find yourself in a better mood? Or smiling more? Or more energetic? Pay close attention. These subtle shifts are all indicators that it is working.

And if a particular affirmation is not really doing anything for you or you feel less and less connected to it over time, then ditch it and try a different one. And if you give this a try and discover this isn't the tool for you, move on. Maybe you'll come back to it down the road when you're in a different place, and you can see if it resonates with you then.

There have been many times in my life when I have tried something out and then stopped only to return to it later when I was more ready to receive what it had for me. For example, for years I hated running. Despised it. Then in my thirties I tried it again and I suddenly found myself settling into a really good meditative rhythm with it and it became one of my favorite exercises. Now, there are people who can walk faster than I run, but so what? Running has become a tool that works for me. So keep affirmations on your tool belt even if you have no use for them right now. They may come in handy one day.

Tool #4—Be Symbolic

In 1999, six years after my brother had been killed, I came out of my house one day and there was a huge red dragonfly splayed out on the sidewalk in front of my car door, perfectly preserved and intact, as if it had been delivered there and then had peacefully passed. I'd been seeing a medicine woman at that time, Sara Urquidez (wife of Benny "the Jet," my kickboxing sensei from above), and she told me that in many cultures around the world, the dragonfly symbolizes change and rebirth—and because the dragonfly was dead, it was surely a message from the spirit world telling me that it was okay to move on and let go of the grief I had been immersed in for years since my brother's death on the set of the film *The Crow*. Whether you believe that or not, it was the right message for me at the right time in my life, and it created a sentiment that I could hold on to because of the prophetic way in which it had all materialized in my path.

Almost ten years later, I decided to take some of the more important symbols of my life and create a tattoo of them, the red dragonfly being one. These symbols, collected together on my body, were a way for me to acknowledge some of the most significant moments of understanding and love in my life. I was almost forty when I got this first and only tattoo—and I'm not recommending you run out and get a tattoo (they're not for everybody), but for me it was a symbolic way to bring me back to myself and the significant moments that had helped shape and heal me.

My father did not have any tattoos, but he believed in symbolism as well, and he used it in his life at seminal moments to create road markers for his journey. He did so through iconography—visual images or symbols that represented his process. Remember the miniature headstone he created? His reminder to the Bruce of yesterday to die and reemerge fluid and expressive once more: *In memory of a once fluid man crammed and distorted by the classical mess.* At the pivotal moments of his life, my father created other symbols to act as concrete reminders of his growth and his new perspectives. He created a series of plaques he called the stages of cultivation to represent the path of his growth, which we will discuss in more depth later. He created his personal symbol for JKD and had a gold pendant made of it to wear every day, as well as a plaque, stationery, cards, certificates, etc. He created a stand with the inspirational words *Walk on!* written on a card to encourage himself to keep moving forward.

Sometimes it's easy to have a revelation and forget to incorporate it into your life. Aha moments are awesome! They feel really good, and while you may think about them often, that doesn't mean you follow through on them and live them proactively. By creating a physically manifested symbol of your revelation, you are, in a way, making an agreement or a statement to be reminded of your new perspective every time you see it. Like a wedding ring you may wear to symbolize your commitment to your partner, you are acknowledging that you are making a commitment to some new path for yourself. You are creating monuments of active encouragement and remembrance that you can return to again and again to keep you invigorated about whatever you have decided you will now embody.

If creating symbols isn't your thing, then consider trying out temporary prompts before you go all the way and build a monument in your yard, get a permanent tattoo, or have gold jewelry designed. There was a period several years back when I had Post-it Notes around my house in key places—on the bathroom mirror, in the kitchen, by my bed—that simply said *BE*. This was my reminder to return to the present moment as often as possible and get out of my own head. It was like a little reset button for me that would bring me back to the here and now, which was usually followed by a sense of calm and clarity (assuming the house wasn't on fire at the moment—haha).

You can also consider creating a ritual. Rituals can be a physical way to acknowledge the passage from one way of being into another. There are all kinds of rituals that already exist—fire rituals, flower rituals, cleansing rituals, etc.—and you can always create your own. The goal of the ritual is for it to resonate with you, so it doesn't matter if you make it up yourself or if you follow someone else's suggestions, as long as it holds meaning for you. I have done burning rituals where I burned items from a past relationship I wanted to let go of, or where I wrote down the patterns that weren't serving me and then burned that piece of paper. Whatever resonates and feels like it will cement the shift you are wishing to create for yourself, do it! Encourage yourself in the best way you know how and make it fun or beautiful or special so that you have a positive, tangible association with the journey ahead.

Tool #5—Journal

In chapter three, we touched on some of my father's writing practices. He wrote often and in many forms. And thank god he did—had it not been for this practice, we wouldn't have been able to understand his process so acutely and clearly. We would not have known about what was important to him, what he was working through, and who he was on a soul level.

When I first started journaling in junior high school, a lot of it was mere gossip. I would write about who I liked and who was bothering me and why what I had done was dumb, but there was almost no information about what my hopes and dreams were. There was no experimentation. I was mostly just recording my moods and my problems. Not that there's anything wrong with that. But if we remember that we strengthen whatever we put our attention on, then that might explain why it took me so long to move on from viewing myself as one big train wreck.

One interesting thing about my father's writings are that there are no negative tirades. That's not to say my father never wrote about anything that was bothering him, but he wrote about it in a way that came with a key realization for himself of what his preferences were—he wrote *through* it. And he landed on what he would like himself or his life to be like instead of what was happening that was "wrong."

For instance, when he was beginning to become very famous in Hong Kong, he started to truly see the adverse effects of fame—people pretending to be his friend for access or favors, the way people glorified famous people but dehumanized everyday people. He wrote in letters to his friends about these trappings, and these insights informed his actions moving forward. He called upon and sought comfort in the voices of old and trusted friends rather than those making lots of promises. He had always considered his move to Hong Kong temporary, and these realizations affirmed the choice to return to Los Angeles as soon as possible, where he could live in more privacy than he was able to in Hong Kong. Unfortunately, he passed away before this could happen.

A journal, or just some loose-leaf papers, can be the place where you discover yourself. I think there is power in handwriting your big thoughts and ideas and processes, but if you prefer to type on the computer, then I would suggest that you read what you write aloud to yourself before filing it away. It can help to connect you to the words in a meaningful way. But regardless of how you write it down, I want to encourage you to do your writing in a way that supports you. Use this time to map out your positive thoughts—what you want, value, believe, wish for, what you're learning and discovering and dreaming about. Work to understand what matters to you, and create a personal vision for yourself. Ask yourself questions and try to answer them. I have tracked dreams for clues. I have listed and described my values. I have contemplated the nature of the universe on paper. My father made many drafts of an essay called "In My Own Process," detailing what was important to him, which I will delve into later. And if you can't think of where to begin, there are many prompts out there in books and online to help get you started.

Now, it can be useful sometimes to do a brain dump. When you are struggling with a lot of toxic thoughts, it can be helpful to rage on the page. So go for it. But rage and then throw that sh*t away. Burn it. Shred it. Don't hang on to it and revisit it. You may think you need to keep it in order to see "how far you've come." But if you've really come far, you will know it. You'll feel different—more calm, more centered, more grounded. You don't need to revisit the past only to be able to pat yourself on the back in the present. Move on and release!

You can track your progress positively. You can note what's trying your patience without fueling it with emotion. My father said it before, and I'll say it again: "Keep your mind on the things you want, and off those you don't." Track your experiments and note your findings. Keep a field journal, a dream journal, an insight journal, a creative journal, a goal journal, but don't keep a bunch of junk that no longer serves you. Let that stuff go.

Tool #6—Get Physical

Bruce Lee was a martial artist. That was his particular physical practice. And whether you think so or not, you need a physical practice too. Not because you need to be an athlete or lose ten pounds. It's not about that. It's about being in touch with your body, knowing how your body feels, and keeping the instrument of your spiritual growth strong. After all, the venerable triumvirate is mind, *body*, spirit.

The art of physical practice is also a way to work on purposefully and literally unbalancing oneself in order to experience some discomfort so that you grow and stretch beyond it. My father said, "To be balanced is to be more or less at rest. Action, then, is the art or method of unbalancing toward keeping oneself moving forward, learning and growing."

We want to understand balance, not only in the mind but in the body. We want to feel what it is to unbalance and then balance, which is what you experience every time you move. Even if all you do is become physically conscious of how you move through space and focus your attention on moving with more strength and/or ease, you will be sensing your body and engaging in physical practice.

Of course, there are all sorts of added benefits to exercise: endorphins, increased strength, increased flexibility, increased confidence, etc. But despite this being a book about a martial artist, that's not what we're focusing on here. We're interested in how a physical practice can help you get to know yourself better. Your body has information for you. It is an intelligent system, replete with networks firing and signals crossing. Feel into it and listen to what it has to say to you when you move it this way and that. Even if you just go for a walk or stretch in front of the TV, put some music on and dance, or do a physically focused meditation where you tense and release parts of your body, one area at a time, you will gain some insight.

The goal in moving your body is to allow yourself to feel something in a safe way. Through even a modicum of vigorous physical movement you can experience what it is to practice discomfort, to experience calculated suffering, and learn to be okay with it. You can use your physical body to push up against some of the edges within yourself. You can learn what it is to work with yourself and not against yourself. It is an invaluable personal discovery tool.

What does your body like? What does it need? Pay attention to your aches and pains. What are they trying to tell you? Get to know your body and how it feels and you will get to the place where you know immediately if something is off internally. This will strengthen and fine tune your intuition and lead to a better understanding of yourself. And you are likely to keep yourself healthier by tuning in to what your body has to say to you.

Just as I use martial arts examples to illustrate philosophical concepts, there is a direct correlation between pushing your body and pushing your soul, stretching your legs and stretching your potential. Remember, my father said that everything he learned about life he learned through the practice of martial arts.

And I do want to take a quick moment to advocate for the practice of martial arts, even just peripherally. Any martial arts training, qi gong, wushu, self-defense classes, or other related styles will enhance your inner strength and your confidence. That's what it did for me. So move your body and see what thoughts, solutions, correlations, obstacles, emotions, and revelations come up.

Imagine and create a physical practice for yourself under the guidelines of communing with your body. Work out like Bruce Lee or be more gentle like me. Nowadays I dance, stretch, walk, run, hit the heavy bag, and hike. Whatever you do, ask your body what it wants and needs; don't be afraid to push it a little and build up your tolerance for discomfort. You'll be surprised how much intelligence and growth is in there.

Embrace the Process

As you go through this process of stretching beyond your comfort zone and putting your ideas and dreams into action, you're going to confront fear and self-doubt. But the difference between people who act and accomplish their goals and people who are left with unfulfilled dreams is that the doers act *alongside* the fear and self-doubt and discomfort.

These tools are not meant to make your life easy—at least not at first. The desire for "easy" often brings out complacency in us. "Easy" can make us lean toward ignorance, laziness, habit, and fear because we don't want life to be too hard or unpredictable and because we fear the discomfort of the unknown and the potential challenging feelings that might arise out of our dark places.

We already heard Bruce say, "The enemy of development is pain phobia—the unwillingness to do a tiny bit of suffering." In order to grow and change, we have to experience discomfort. Your muscles don't get stronger without being broken down first (that's what sore-ness is—tiny tears in the muscle before it rebuilds). The first few days in the gym are always the most challenging, and then there are the pla-teaus. But let's not frame life as "easy" or "hard" but rather as *alive,* al-ways growing, always changing. Approach this growth and change with enthusiasm rather than anxiety. And remember to tap into the energy of the big dreams to keep you going when the going gets tough, and to learn from your setbacks.

As I mentioned before, people grow by skillful frustrations. If you were never frustrated by something, you would never seek a solution to your frustration. And in our water practice, the goal is to create *skillful,* intentional frustrations. It's much better to choose your frus-trations rather than get blindsided by them. And you don't become good at running marathons without first suffering through running a mile and then three miles and then five miles and then ten and so on and so on. That's what we want—a skillful plan. Don't go out and try to run 26.2 miles all in one go never having run before. We want to set up a training plan that builds us up toward growth, step by step, so we have the space to be resilient when mistakes happen.

Over time, as we practice and nourish our best growth, the jour-ney itself becomes joyful because of how alive we feel in the midst of it. And then we become accepting of the lessons that will come from any difficulties we experience, and we stop living so much for the outcomes. Yes, we may need to process some hard stuff and make some tough choices in our lives, but learning to love the process and appreciate the possibilities as we move forward will allow us to let go of our doubt and fear and worry and begin to see the limitlessness of our potential.

My father was a person who had goals. Goals are important. Knowing what our goals are gives us something to work toward. They shape our forward motion and create the framework for our training.

It's important to remember, though, that goals are not the be-all and end-all. In fact, when we tend to get fixated on accomplishing our goals, we often miss the journey entirely—only to find that when we reach our goal, there's now yet another goal we want to go for. At that point, it's hard to acknowledge our progress, and we start to feel like we are never going to get there (wherever "there" is). It's like holding the next bite of food in your hand while you're still chewing the first one—you're so anxious for what's next, you end up missing the meal altogether.

But goals are still incredibly useful as long as we don't forget to be present and fluid with them. My father would, in fact, encourage you to set goals and to make at least one definite move daily toward them. He would suggest that to strive actively to achieve some goal will, in fact, give your life meaning and substance. But he would also caution that a goal is not always meant to be reached. Rather it simply serves as something to lean into, a future to live toward. The point, really, is in the doing and not in the outcomes. The maximizing of one's potential is not the tallying of accomplishments, but the continual engagement in life as a process of unlimited growth.

> All goals apart from the means are an illusion. There
> will never be means to ends, only means. And I am
> means. I am what I started with, and when it is all over,
> I will be all that is left of me. You can employ a sys-
> tematic approach to training and practicing but never
> employ a method to living. Life is a process, not a goal;
> a means but not an end; a constant movement rather
> than an established pattern.

I love this: "I am means." I am the process. I am the life that will one day come to its end. My life is happening right now and there's no "someday" or "if then" or "but when." I am the method of my life. I am the creator of my life. I am the tool for my living. My body, my mind, my spirit are all at my disposal toward whatever I want to do, to believe, and to expand upon. So live your life like this is your life to live. Because it is.

Start Right Now

The tools we touched on—goal-setting, taking action, affirmations, symbolism, journaling, physical practice, and meditation (chapter two)—are just a few of the tangible ways my father cultivated his potential. I'm sure you can devise even more tools that will work especially well for you and you alone as you gain confidence and begin to really know yourself and what your potential holds. My father did that—if he didn't have the equipment he wanted, he made it.

So just begin. You don't have to have all the answers to begin. Sometimes you have to begin in order to find the answers you are looking for. And you may have to get really creative in the cultivation of your tools, or you may need to lean into something you thought you'd never give any credence to, like energy work or dharma practices or herbalism. Some of us have some serious stuff to unpack and deal with and the task may feel daunting. Now is the time to act, learn, create, and align your words with your deeds. Or stop talking and get busy doing.

> In this world there are a lot of people who talk intellectually about how they would do this or do that. They talk about it but nothing is ever actualized or accomplished.

Remember, you are means. And you are in a process of discovery and growth. As my father believed:

> When you drop a pebble into a pool of water, the pebble starts a series of ripples that expand until they encompass the whole pool. This is exactly what will happen when I give my ideas a definite plan of action.

Trust yourself. Trust the process. And begin.

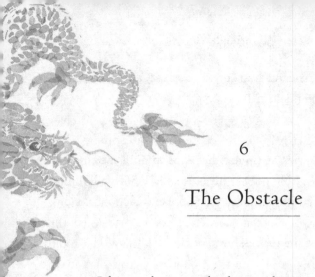

6

The Obstacle

Believe me that in every big thing or achievement there are always obstacles, big or small, and the reaction one shows to such obstacles is what counts, not the obstacle itself. There is no such thing as defeat until you admit it to yourself, but not until then!

A Not So Good Morning

In 1964, my father did a demonstration at the Long Beach International Karate Championship. He spoke about Chinese gung fu and demonstrated some of his showstopping techniques on students and volunteers. His charisma caught the eye of Jay Sebring, Hollywood hairdresser to the stars, who was in the audience—and whose producer client had recently been talking to him about a show that needed an Asian actor. Jay left the tournament mesmerized by this young Bruce Lee kid and called his client, William Dozier, to tell him about my father.

Some time later, back at their home in Oakland, the phone rang and my mother answered. When the man on the line identified himself as a Hollywood producer looking for her husband, she thought it might be some kind of practical joke. She gave Bruce the message and when he called back, he was asked to come down to Los Angeles for a Hollywood screen test.

My father made his way from Oakland to LA just days after the birth of their first child, my brother, Brandon, and auditioned for a show about Charlie Chan's Number One Son. He wowed the room, and although plans for *Number One Son* were ultimately sidelined, the producer loved Bruce so much that he paid to hold him until he could cast him in another project. He was soon offered the role of Kato in *The Green Hornet*.

The Green Hornet and Kato were a crime-fighting duo who took on a host of villains week to week. My father was cast in the sidekick role, but there was no hiding how much of a badass he was, and soon the inequity between the Green Hornet's crime-fighting skills and Kato's became obvious, to fans at least. Unfortunately (or fortunately, perhaps), the TV show *Batman* had hit the airwaves at the same time as *The Green Hornet* and proved to be much more popular, and *The Green Hornet* was canceled after only one season.

But something life-altering had already taken place. My father saw how showcasing his gung fu in a mass entertainment venue was lining up with his clearly stated life's purpose: he was letting the world know of the greatness of his Chinese art. He began to think that if he could originate his own projects, he could bring an authentic portrayal of a Chinese man and Chinese art to the silver screen, and he would be helping and teaching people at the same time. He saw how a career in Hollywood, if he were successful, might also provide a good income for his family. Many boxes could be checked on the grand vision!

I imagine he could see this newly adjusted goal painted across the canvas of his mind just as clearly as the chain of schools he had once imagined, and being a practical dreamer, he didn't just close up shop and put all his eggs in the Hollywood basket. He continued to open schools, opening his third in Los Angeles in 1967, and he taught privately at home and at other people's homes while he looked for more opportunities in film and television, and began trying to create some media opportunities of his own.

Between the years of 1966 and 1971, my father worked tirelessly to make it in Hollywood. After *The Green Hornet* went off air, it was hard for an Asian man to springboard into a starring role (or even a meaty supporting role). And my father refused to take roles that were demeaning portrayals of Asians, making the opportunities even fewer for him. He'd been the second lead on a TV series, but he wasn't considered a bankable star. Still, he auditioned as much as he could, and was able to land small parts in film and on TV. He played Asian kung fu guys in *Ironside, Here Comes the Bride,* and *Marlowe,* and took on jobs in fight choreography as well.

One of his students was writer Stirling Silliphant, with whom he sometimes collaborated and worked to hone his creative ideas as well. Another student was Ted Ashley, the head of Warner Brothers Studio, to whom he pitched a number of projects and tried to get support. And all the while, he continued to train and teach, while maintaining three schools in Seattle, Oakland, and Los Angeles. In other words, he was doing everything he knew how to do. He was working hard and straight up hustling.

By mid-1970, my father's career seemed to be moving in the right direction. He had pitched the film *The Silent Flute* to Warner Brothers and they were considering it as a possibility, and he had just pitched a TV series called *The Warrior* to Warner Brothers as well. He was hopeful that he was on his way to truly fulfilling his goals, but it was taking a long time, and success was elusive and distant. So he kept up his training and his teaching and his Hollywood-ing so that he was always ready to avail himself of any opportunity that came along.

One morning my father was getting ready to work out at home, where he typically trained. He trained outside in the backyard, which is possible most days of the year in Southern California. He had his own weights and training equipment, such as punching bags set up under the eve on the back patio—no fancy gym for him.

On this particular day he had a lot on his plate, and having already cultivated a certain level of fitness, he figured he could skip his warm-up. He started off with something called a Good Morning exercise, where you place a weighted barbell across the tops of your shoulders and, while holding the bar steady, bend at the waist and lean forward with a straight back as far as you can go (face to knees if you can), and then pull yourself back up in a similar fashion all while shouldering this weight, which, if you knew my father, was likely to have been very heavy. It's very difficult to do (and should not be attempted unless you already have proper experience and training). He brought the barbell down, and when he began to rise, he felt a twinge and a pop in his back. He knew immediately that something bad had happened.

As the day progressed, his back worsened, and he couldn't stand up straight or move without pain. He tried resting it and treating it as an athlete would (ice, balms, etc.), but the pain would not subside and his mobility was seriously impinged. So he sought out a doctor for a diagnosis. The doctor told him he'd injured his fourth sacral nerve quite seriously, and ordered him to bed rest. That, alone, would be bad news for an active person like my father, who made his livelihood through his physicality, but there was more bad news to come. The doctor told him he would have to prepare for the idea that he would never do martial arts again, and that he may, in fact, never walk again without considerable pain.

Not just bad news—devastating news. Not only would he not be able to work in Hollywood with this kind of injury, he couldn't train or teach as effectively either. Enter . . . the obstacle.

It's Not the Obstacle That Matters

> It is not a shame to be knocked down. The important thing is to ask when you're being knocked down, "why am I being knocked down?" If a person can reflect in this way, then there is hope for this person. Defeat is a state of mind; no one is ever defeated until defeat has been accepted as a reality. To me, defeat in anything is merely temporary, and its punishment is but an urge for me to exert greater effort to achieve my goal. Defeat simply tells me that something is wrong in my doing; it is a path leading to success and truth.

Obstacles come in all shapes and sizes and levels of intensity. Some are momentary obstacles—you procrastinate too much and now you might fail your exam, or your car broke down and you are going to miss a big meeting. Others are more chronic and serious—you may have an addiction problem or struggle with clinical depression. Still others can come out of nowhere—you may have been in a car accident or a pipe burst in your apartment. Obstacles are a given. You will never *not* encounter them. Some may be of your own making, your own choices, and some just land on you. Whatever the situation, it's best to try to remember that the obstacle is just "what happened." It is neutral in this way. It is what has occurred. And it's what you make of "what happened" that makes all the difference.

Of course, there will be initial shock and plenty of emotions. You might be upset or numb or depressed. Allow yourself this. But try not to get stuck there for overlong. Many people don't get past an obstacle because they get caught in the devastation of it and become defeated. But when a seemingly devastating event occurs, it's crucial to get to the next step of: Now what?

> In everyday life the mind is capable of moving from one thought to one object to another. However, when one is face to face with an opponent in a deadly contest, the mind tends to lose its mobility and get sticky and stopped. This is a problem that haunts everyone.

The opponent in this case is the obstacle. When we hit a big roadblock, it's easy not only to get stuck but to lose hope. My father said, "It is not what happens that is success or failure, but what it does to the heart of man." What does it do to your heart? Will you let it defeat you? Or will you learn to use it to step into something new? Something unexpected? Perhaps even something better?

When it comes to a new obstacle, start off by just sitting with it. Be with it. Cozy up to it. Learn from it. What has it got to show you? To teach you? How will you have to change to move beyond it? What new skill will you have to learn? What old wound might you need to heal? When you get in the ring and you keep getting punched in the face, do you learn how to duck and cover and eventually learn how to hit back? Or do you just stand there and keep letting yourself get punched in the face until you go down and never get back up?

You have a choice in how you respond to anything that happens in your life. You may think that you don't, but you *always* do. Remember, first and foremost, that a response is also an inward state of being. You may be conditioned to respond in a particular way, and that conditioning may seem ironclad, natural, and unquestionable to you, but it's always just one option no matter how ingrained. No matter what happens to you, you hold the power to determine what comes next. You are in charge of your reaction, and in this way, you are all powerful.

> Remember, my friend, it's not what happens that counts; it is how you react. Your mental attitude determines what you make of it, either a stepping stone or a stumbling block.

Walk On

There my father was: an elite athlete with big plans and dreams that are suddenly in jeopardy of being lost forever. How did he respond? Well, first, he was upset. Naturally. But my mother always said that after a big shake-up, my father would typically get very quiet. He would sort of retreat into himself for a while to sit with the problem. In this instance, he began his process by following the first natural steps before him—taking care of his body by resting and going to the doctor. *Then*, once he had had time to masticate on the situation a bit, he would go into research mode (see chapter three!). He spoke to doctors; he bought books on back pain; he tested his pain and range of motion slowly and methodically. In my father's library to this day are numerous books on healing back pain.

Being Bruce Lee and valuing time, he also wasn't going to just lie in bed and do nothing even while he was "resting." So, aside from reading and researching, he also wrote. With ample time on his hands, he began to record his thoughts on martial arts for posterity and clarity. He began a work he called his *Commentaries on the Martial Way*, a seven-volume tome that expressed his thoughts on combat and training. He worked on creative ideas as well—more film and television ideas. He continued to teach from the sidelines. Students would come to the house and he would sit in a chair to instruct them. He just kept going—doing what he could do and using his time purposefully.

He also read what we would call "self-help" books during this time—books that helped cultivate a powerful mindset and positive attitude, such as *Happiness Begins Before Breakfast* by Harry and Joan Mier, *The Art of Loving* by Erich Fromm, *Anxiety: A Condition of Modern Man* by Heiri Steiner and Jean Gebser, *Give Yourself a Chance: Seven Steps to Success* by Gordon Byron, *Joy: Expanding Human Awareness* by William C. Schutz, and the list went on and on. It was during this time that my father, the man of intention and symbol-maker that he was, grabbed one of his business cards and wrote in his big, beautiful script on the back (and with a big fat exclamation point after it): *Walk On!* He had a wooden stand made for the card, and he put it on display before him so that he could see it every day from where he recuperated. Whenever he was down or frustrated, he had a reminder to: Just. Keep. Going. Just keep doing your work, one step at a time, one moment at a time—even if you're not sure where it will ultimately lead.

I see *Walk On!* and it reminds me of Dory from *Finding Nemo* saying in her singsong voice, "Just keep swimming. Just keep swimming. Swimming. Swimming." It doesn't matter how long it will take to get better (whether that's mentally, emotionally, or physically). If you never start, you will never get there. If you let fear or being upset stop you and you retreat into paralysis, then you most definitely will never get there. And let's say you spend the next ten years just walking forward in your progress a tiny bit, one millimeter at a time—well, at some point you will be able to look back and see the miles of progress. But not if you don't keep going. If you stay in one spot, the view never changes, but if you keep moving forward, then new landscapes are revealed, and along with them, new potential.

Life is an ever-flowing process and somewhere on the path some unpleasant things will pop up—it might leave a scar, but then life flows on, and like running water, if it stops, it grows stale. Go bravely on, my friend because each experience teaches us a lesson. Keep blasting because life is such that sometimes it is nice and sometimes not.

Don't Blunt the Tools

So here you are, faced with a need to dig into your toolbox because you've just encountered an obstacle. And you now know that you have to compel yourself to walk on—keep moving forward. But knowing all this and doing it are two very different things, and the first big differentiating factor is your state of mind.

> If you think a thing is impossible, you'll make it impossible. Pessimism blunts the tools you need to succeed.

I often tell my daughter when she is stressing out about an exam that all the complaining and groaning and worrying is just making it harder to study. The studying is already hard enough. She doesn't have to like the studying, but if she wants to do the best she can, then studying is an important factor. So I tell her to try as best she can to take the layer of negative emotions and pessimistic thoughts off the task at hand and move it to neutral. You are the creator and the interpreter of your life in every moment. Things have meaning to you because *you* give them that meaning—no one else. Even if the meaning you are using came from someone else (your parents, your pastor, etc.), you still chose to adopt this meaning and use it. You are in charge.

If someone insults me, I can choose to be insulted, or I can choose to hold that person in compassion because they are obviously struggling with something themselves, or I can choose to express myself to them, or I can choose to walk away. I can choose to make that insult mean that the world is a terrible place or I can choose to make it mean that there's a lot of healing to do in the world and wonder how I can do my part. I am the creator of my experience. I get to choose.

Worry doesn't solve a problem; it makes a problem out of the problem. Pessimism doesn't solve a problem; it makes a problem harder by implying it is impossible to solve. Fear doesn't solve a problem; it stops us from attacking the problem because we are afraid of failing or making the problem worse. Doubt doesn't solve a problem; it gives you an excuse not to solve the problem. And apathy doesn't solve a problem; it leaves you uncaring about anything at all. All this negativity just blunts the tools you have at your disposal to overcome an obstacle. It creates obstacles in front of obstacles.

Realize that you are powerful. Don't give your agency to others or to negativity or to circumstance. Don't hinder your abilities. Your world has no meaning except for the meaning you give it, and maybe there's no need to give it any meaning. Stepping stones or stumbling blocks—the choice is yours. Consider this realization like my father did:

> I've always been buffeted by circumstance because I thought of myself as a human being influenced by outside conditioning. Now I realize that I am the power that commands the feeling of my mind from which circumstances grow.

Be a Nobody

During this time of the back injury, my father was laid up. My parents had two small children (four years old and six months old). To make matters worse, they had just bought their first house and now were risking being unable to pay the mortgage because my father couldn't work. My mother had to take a job answering a switchboard late at night while my father tried to put two small children to bed with a back injury. My father was embarrassed that his wife had to take a job to make ends meet, but what else could they do? If they were going to make it through this, he was going to have to swallow some pride, and they'd have to figure it out.

If my father had injured his back and thought to himself, "I'm Bruce Lee. I can't have a back injury!" then he might have tried too hard to push himself back to health too soon and injured himself more in the process. He might have become despondent, feeling like he could no longer "live up to" the person he and everyone else thought he was while his family lost their home. He might never have gone on to make movies in Hong Kong. He would have been that guy on that sixties show *The Green Hornet* that lasted one season, and we would never have had much reason to revisit that part of his career because that would have been it. A blip on the screen of pop culture.

But because he was a person who believed in research, inquiry, experimentation, and taking control of his own destiny, he was able to ask himself: What can I learn from this obstacle? How can I move forward from here and encourage myself to keep going? Rather than leaning into some outside, idealized version of his identity, my father was able to take a step back and assess this challenge.

And he had one more cultivated ability at his disposal. An important component of being a highly skilled martial artist is an absolute sensitivity for timing. In a battle against a skilled opponent (or obstacle), you can only progress and strike at the appropriate time. If you strike too early, you may get blocked or parried or not reach the target at all. If you strike too late, your target may not be there anymore or may have already popped you a good one.

Dealing with an obstacle requires this discipline. Push yourself too hard, and you may flame out. Don't push yourself hard enough, and you may never get there. Bruce Lee, hot-tempered, fiery man of action that he was, had impeccable timing. And part of that timing was the development of patience. Yes, he struggled with this given his temperament. But here's what he said about patience: "Patience is not passive. On the contrary, patience is concentrated strength." Think about the back injury. He needed to patiently and appropriately rest, research, and approach his recovery with the best timing and effort for the best outcome. Too much activity too soon and he would risk reinjury.

Sometimes it takes all you have just to wait. Can you see how for a man of action like my father, the implementation of patience would take so much concentrated strength? I myself am a "tackle the problem" kind of person, but sometimes, in the face of a great obstacle, we need to pause and check in with ourselves, with the timing, with what we're being shown. We have to engage all our senses and remove our egos from the picture in order to move forward appropriately and in a way that gets us around that obstacle permanently.

> One should get rid of the obtruding self and apply himself to the work to be done as if nothing particular were taking place at the moment. Use the ego as a tool rather than a possession. Inwardly, psychologically, be a nobody.

When we are powerful enough to assign our own meaning to the world, we don't need to make up a story about what kind of person we might be in the eyes of others. We don't have to follow anyone else's expectations about overcoming obstacles. Instead try on the concept of being a nobody. What does that mean? It means check your ego at the door and don't let your definition of self-importance or self-protection get in the way of your progress around obstacles.

By allowing himself to be a nobody inwardly—not "the great martial artist and star Bruce Lee" but just another guy, with a bad back, trying to live life to his fullest and do something with his time while he has it—Bruce Lee was able to become a somebody who most of us will never forget.

Spiritual Willpower

Beyond being a nobody, overcoming obstacles requires harnessing willpower. As my father said, "The spiritual power of man's will removes all obstacles." And you may remember that in one of my father's affirmations he wrote, "The power of will is the supreme court over all other departments of my mind." My father considered himself a "self-willed" man. Now, this is not the be-all and end-all of one's existence because, as you are seeing, there are times when other sensitivities are necessary beyond willpower. But in the pantheon of action and purpose, my father considered himself fully weaponized, not only because he was a skilled fighter and in peak shape, but because he knew how to harness his will.

Harnessing my will is what I have to do to make myself sit down and write this book or eat well or work out or deal with my issues and problems. Sometimes I'm simply inspired to write and eat well and work out and grow. But if I always relied on a need to be fully inspired to act on my own behalf, I would hardly ever do so, and it would be super inconsistent. It's much easier to be lazy and ignorant and feel justified all the time.

Do you want me to make an argument about why I should eat whatever I want every day, no matter how bad it is for me? Okay, here you go: Why shouldn't I always have delicious, fatty, sugary, salty food in my mouth every time I eat? It makes me happy. Isn't life about being happy? And feeling good? Well, this is what makes me happy and feel good.

But then, the counterargument is that it really only makes me feel good while I'm eating it, and it really only makes some limited version of me feel good and happy, because I don't feel good and happy when my body feels like crap later. For a brief moment I think, "Yum!" And then eventually, I feel horrible, physically and mentally. See the problem?

So yes, we need to use our willpower, but *how* are we using it? Are we using it to manage and maintain a façade or even multiple façades? Or are we using it in the long game of our lives—in service to our personal growth? As my father posited:

> What is will? It is the attempt to direct one's energy
> within the unlimited unfolding of the universe in order
> to join in harmony with this unfolding in the direction
> of one's doing.

By this definition, your will is not an isolated thing that you harness alone. Rather, it takes into consideration the unfolding of everything around you such that you can direct your actions in concert with all that is happening. You know the phrase "Go with the flow"? If you are not taking this more holistic approach to willpower but rather just pushing hard against the flow of things with your determination, then you are giving yourself a much harder time. You may be able to paddle upstream for a little while, but try to travel the entire length of the Mississippi this way. You're going to gas out eventually.

Let's look back at "should-ing." Using one's willpower in service of "should" is not using it spiritually and will not remove the obstacle. I "should" eat healthily and I can "force" myself to do so. But that is not connecting me to anything purposeful. It is using guilt to make me submit. Now, if I use my will to eat healthily because I have a vision for a long life and a strong body and because it will make the accomplishing of all my other goals easier because I will feel good and have lots of energy, well, *that* is the spiritual use of my will. In that scenario, I am taking into consideration the whole picture and infusing the path with positivity. I am directing my energy and my doing in harmony with the unfolding of the big vision I have for my life.

Just as my father harnessed his will during the time of his back trauma to not only recuperate, research, and strategize his recovery, but also to continue the pursuit of his goals and dreams by reading and writing, we can use our wills to accomplish our goals while nourishing our souls. The intentional and beneficial ways in which we use our time lie at the root of sustaining our spirits and realizing ourselves. As my father said, "If you love life, don't waste time, for time is what life is made up of."

Re-owning the Dream

All accomplishment starts from a place of deciding that what you want to accomplish is possible. Remember the practical dream? For Elon Musk, going to space is possible. For Bruce Lee, being the first Asian leading man in a feature film in 1960s Hollywood was possible. Whatever it is, don't discount it just because it may be big, take a long time, and you're not exactly sure how you're going to get there. Believing your dream is possible is a key factor when facing the obstacles that will inevitably appear along the path—and a necessary component in overcoming them.

Now, I want to tell you something you might not know. My father had back pain for the rest of his life. He wasn't able to magically cure himself of all back pain through his will and positivity. But you know what he was able to do? He was able to strengthen and heal his body to the point where the weakness in his back was supported by the surrounding muscles and the overall health of the rest of his body. Following his injury, he always took lots of time to warm up and cool down. He cared for his back constantly with ice and heat as needed after workouts. He took Western and Eastern pain relief medications as needed. And he learned how to train and teach and act and perform with his bad back.

More important, he didn't let the injury define him or stop him or cancel out his dreams. All of the movies he made in which he is shredded into the best shape of his life and kicking ass left and right, he did with this weak back. And it took more time for him to be able to do those things because of the care he had to give his back, but that's what it required and so that is what he did to achieve his dream.

> I mean, who has the most insecure job as I have? What do I live on? My faith in my ability that I'll make it. Sure my back screwed me up good for a year but with every adversity comes a blessing because a shock acts as a reminder to oneself that we must not get stale in routine. With adversity you are shocked to higher levels if you allow yourself to go beyond your current circumstances.

When the dream starts to fall apart or the formula we are using stops working, this can be a time of crisis. Or this can be a time of coming back to oneself, back to your dream, back to your clarity. It can be a time to reassess and maybe dream anew. It can be a time to purposefully empty your cup, unclutter your thoughts and emotions, and make space for something you haven't considered before. And if the clarity, vision, and purpose of your dreams are still there for you, even in the face of big obstacles, then it is time to pick up the pieces of the dream and reassemble them. Same vision, different shape perhaps. Or newly clarified vision, even more defined shape. Whatever the configuration . . .

> Put the different fragments of the dream together and re-own these fragmented parts; re-own the hidden potential in the dream. As we progress and time changes, it is often necessary to reform the formula.

There is always something to learn if you look closely—and especially from within our obstacles. Our obstacles are among some of our greatest teachers. They will show us how to benefit most from our strengths and our weaknesses. They will open us up to new realms of understanding and help us develop new skills if we allow them to do so.

> Do what seems wise to be done, forget it and walk on. Walk on and see a new view. Walk on and see the birds fly. Walk on and leave behind all things that would dam up the inlet or clog the outlet of experience.

Sometimes we are sent on a whole life journey we never intended to go on, specifically because we rose to the occasion of what our lives threw at us. In the case of my father, he was able to work with his obstacle and stay on his path. A boulder fell into his stream, and his stream adapted and kept on flowing. But for some of us, the changes life throws at us can be unfathomable. An obstacle is one thing. It's a problem, maybe even a big problem. But what about when life stops making sense altogether. What then?

7

The Rainstorm

No matter what, you must let your inner light
guide you out of the darkness.

Sometimes the obstacle before you is so vast that you can't even see it for what it is. It's not just a problem; it's an existential crisis. Your life is altered so completely and so unexpectedly that you become lost. You feel as if you are in the middle of a raging storm, adrift in a large sea with nothing for miles around but giant, engulfing waves. There's a tsunami heading your way, and there was never any warning.

Chaos

On March 31, 1993, I was asleep in my bed in New Orleans when I received a phone call in the middle of the night from my mom. She told me that there had been an accident on the set of my brother's film and that Brandon had been injured. I was to fly to Atlanta to meet her, and from there we would fly on together to Wilmington, North Carolina, where he was. She had bought me the plane ticket but didn't have much more information than that.

I packed a bag without understanding what I was packing a bag for, and went to the airport in the predawn hours that morning. I flew to meet my mom and at our layover we heard more news. Something about his aorta having been damaged. They were working on him. This didn't sound good, but no one was saying how serious it really was.

We boarded the plane to Wilmington and were separated on the plane because of our last-minute tickets. I was sitting in my seat in a state of mild panic and anxiety, flying through the air thousands of feet above the ground—and suddenly I felt this bolt shoot through me, like a beam of energy that passed through the plane, through my body and out the top. It was powerful and completely disconcerting. I burst into tears because in that moment I knew that my brother had died. I had felt his spirit exiting his body through my own. That's all it could have been. I don't know how to convey this other than that I knew it to be true. After a minute, I fought back the tears, working to convince myself that I was wrong. How could I know that was what was going on? I started rationalizing and explaining to myself that I was just stressed and being ridiculous.

We landed in Wilmington and exited the plane onto the tarmac where we were met by my brother's fiancé. My mom went to her and they embraced. My brother's fiancé spoke to my mother briefly while holding her, and then I watched as my mother collapsed to the ground, her knees buckling. I was right. My brother was dead.

From there all I could feel was nothing. I was crying but inside I was in shock. We got in the car and headed to the hospital to see his body, a horrifying experience, as he didn't look at all like himself after so many hours of surgery and fluids. The rest was chaos. A descent into the wilds of life. Map-less terrain with no understanding of the landscape.

Now you may think that I had gone through this before because my father died when I was young. And I had indeed. But I was only four then, and what I remember of that was a much more vague confusion and chaos, the imprint of a sea of grieving humanity in Hong Kong as thousands lined the streets for his funeral. The grief of my mother and my brother. And the turn inward on myself. But that's all. I didn't even know the word *grief*. I don't remember my own grieving. I had unconsciously and mercifully cordoned that off from my memory.

But here I was twenty years later and grief was thrust upon me like a wild animal. We stayed in North Carolina for some days (I couldn't tell you if it was two or four), then flew to Seattle to bury my brother next to my father. Then we flew to Los Angeles, where a memorial was held. Somewhere in there my birthday happened. My body was there for all of it, but it was like I was in some weird dream where the sights and sounds were blurry and muted, and I couldn't feel anything except overwhelming sadness and cognitive dissonance.

Eventually I ended up back in New Orleans, back to where I'd been living, but without a brother in the world anymore. How was I meant to carry on? The universe was nonsensical. It felt as if there was no discernable meaning to anything anymore. I was standing in the middle of the storm—a tsunami on one side, a tornado barreling down on the other, and an earthquake beneath my feet.

I knew how to go through each day, but I no longer knew how to live. I had already made a plan to move back to LA at the end of the summer to live near my brother and start an acting career. I had talked to him about it before he started filming *The Crow* (the film on which he was killed). After he died, I arrived back in New Orleans without a job and a few months to pass before moving to California as planned, and so I took a job painting dorm rooms on the campus at Tulane University. It was perfect because I didn't really need to speak to anyone. I could just listen to music and paint for eight hours a day, rolling cinder-block walls in the suffocating Louisiana summer heat.

One day, while I was rolling paint, my own knees buckled and I suddenly sank to the floor. It was a feeling of collapse—like a person who has been gripping a bar trying to hold themselves up for as long as they can and their body finally just gives out. I sat there breathing like I was breathing for the first time, and I realized I had been holding my breath for months. That was the beginning of the torrent of grief for me. The dam had finally broken.

I moved to LA at the end of the summer as planned, and for the first time in my life I became afraid of casual things, like turbulence on an airplane or making conversation with people. I was in constant pain, sometimes unable to get up in the morning, get dressed, or move off my couch for hours at a time. I would cry as I drove around LA in my car. On the inside, I was in trouble, but on the outside, I was going through each day, trying to start an acting career, living with my boyfriend, going through the motions of life. All the while, I was dumbfounded and confused as to how I was supposed to ever feel good again, how I was supposed to make sense of the world.

I remember that, at the time, I wished I'd been raised in a faith that had an explanation I could grab hold of for why this had happened or where my brother's soul was or what I was supposed to do now. I had no context for these events. And that's not to say that I wished for a religious context. I just wished I believed in something that would provide a structure for all this torrent.

I existed in this way for years. I got married. I started a career. I made a home. All on the outside. But inside, I was shut down. The rainstorm was still coming on strong, and I was drowning.

My father said, "What is the opposite of existence? The immediate answer might be 'nonexistence' but this is incorrect. The opposite is 'anti-existence.'"

Nonexistence is just a barren nothing, while anti-existence is a devout resistance to living. This period was in a lot of ways an anti-existence for me. I was existing but I didn't feel alive. I was going through each day, but I was just going through the motions. I had made plans and chosen paths, but I was on autopilot. I wasn't truly embodying my career or my marriage or my life. And I imagine that's the way a lot of people feel, whether they've had a tragedy or a traumatic event befall them or not. Just going through life, not fully sure why, not fully engaged, shut down internally, maybe knowing there's something missing or something better but not sure what to do about it.

The Medicine

It was coincidentally about this time that some books of my father's writings were being contemplated for publishing, and so all his writings had been gathered up and given to me to look at and go through. I wasn't running the business then; the writings had just been given to me as a courtesy. My brother had been gone a couple of years at this point and life was moving along. I took these stacks and stacks of my father's words and began going through them. I saw the ones I had always known—"Be water, my friend"; "Using no way as way, having no limitation as limitation," etc. And then I came across a quote that hit me square in the chest. It said:

> The medicine for my suffering I had within me from
> the very beginning, but I did not take it. My ailment

came from within myself, but I did not observe it until this moment. Now I see that I will never find the light unless, like the candle, I am my own fuel, consuming myself.

I don't know why this spoke so clearly to me in this moment, and I didn't really know what to do with it. But I felt, for the first time, what can only be described as hope. As though someone had given me a clue to a giant puzzle that I didn't even know I had been trying to solve.

I began to recognize that I'd been repeating over and over to myself, not proactively, not with great intention or purpose, but really in utter desperation, this internal plea: "Help me. I can't live like this. Please help me." And the first cracks of light came through in this reading of my father's words. Somehow I had unconsciously called help to me and help had arrived.

So often we feel like the answer to our pain is to ignore it or expunge it, to let it go without acknowledging it because to do so would be to potentially implode. But I was already suffering so much, and here was my father saying to me that I had the medicine to cure myself. Did I really? How? Further quotes revealed thoughts like, "Let yourself go with the disease, be with it, keep company with it; this is the way to get rid of it." And, "In the middle of chaos lies opportunity."

I had been thrown into the maelstrom of chaos and had become rigid, so gripped by my pain that I could barely breathe. I was resisting life while pretending at life, because I couldn't believe that life could be good anymore. How could life be good again with a dead brother on top of a dead father? There was no logical path forward to true happiness from here. But this existence I was cowering inside of was no life either and so I succumbed. I looked inward. I wanted to live my father's words. I wanted to believe that there was more.

I began to seek to order my chaos. I sat with my grief and I sought more books, more words, therapists, healers. I opened myself up to the grief of loss and let it teach me how to live. I delved deeper into my father's philosophy, and I began to seek out being more purposeful, more real, more whole. And it's still happening. I am a work in progress—as we all are. I have sometimes been lulled back to sleep and disengaged from life by the choices and mistakes I continue to make. I still struggle, but, in that moment, for the first time in my life, I began to know there was something more. I began to glimpse the possibility of joy and freedom. I began to realize through my seeking that within me lay dormant the capacity for aliveness that I had forgotten so long ago. In coming to terms with the reality of my life, I realized that I had been mildly depressed most of my life, from the time of my father's death until I finally got free of that chronic depression around the age of thirty. In my ignorance I thought that everyone felt the kind of soul pain that I had always felt. I just thought that was how life was for everyone.

My father said, "With adversity you are shocked to higher levels, much like a rainstorm that is so violent, but yet afterwards all the plants grow." By taking my healing into my own hands and searching unrelentingly for wholeness, I had come to discover his truth and make it my own. I had made it through the rainstorm and discovered a whole new life on the other side that was in full bloom. I came to cultivate a faith in the journey that I had not previously had. And life started to disclose its secrets to me.

My father's words had struck the match and offered that first light for me. Like the candle, I began to burn. And, slowly, the clouds began to lift and the whole world began to light up.

> We are always in a process of becoming and nothing is
> fixed. Have no rigid system in you, and you'll be flexible

to change with the ever changing. Open yourself and flow, my friend. Flow in the total openness of the living moment. If nothing within you stays rigid, outward things will disclose themselves. Moving, be like water. Still, be like a mirror. Respond like an echo.

When you stop resisting life—even the hard parts of life—then you start to be a part of life, and life takes you under its wing and says to you, "Look. This is how we live." And after a time, you realize you are ready to stop swirling around and around in that little eddy at the riverbank because you know yourself to be the stream, and it becomes safe to let yourself flow forth again.

Leap of Faith

I wanted to tell you this story because you may feel like life is kind of meh—or worse, you may feel like life is painful and grinding you down. If so, then you are in the rainstorm and you may not realize it. Like me in my twenty-six year malaise of depression, you may be shut down and not even know it. You don't have to be able to pinpoint a traumatic event in your life like I did to know that you are not truly living. If you can't possibly imagine feeling vibrant and full of energy most of the time, I am here to tell you that you're not alone—and I'm here to tell you that kind of alive life is *not* just a fantasy for hippies and superheroes. It's possible. Just because you haven't been able to access it yet doesn't mean that you can't. But you have to decide to believe that you can have it, and then you have to pursue it. You have to make that leap of faith.

My father said, "I cannot and will not scoff at faith when reason seems to be such a barren thing." And what is faith? By his definition,

"Faith is the maintaining of the soul through which one's aims may be translated into their physical equivalent." Faith maintains the soul. To me that means trusting in the things that make me feel whole. Furthermore, my father believed:

> Faith is a state of mind that can be conditioned through self-discipline. Faith can be induced or created by re-peated instructions to the subconscious mind through the principle of autosuggestion. This is the voluntary development of the emotion of faith.

Let's break that down. Faith means believing or trusting. So while there is reason, logic, evidence, deduction, analysis, etc., there's also trusting oneself, trusting others who have your back, trusting the journey, believing in one's instincts and intuition. Intuition is the language of the soul. It points us toward our heart's expression. Intuition is that sensation or signal you receive to explore or follow something even when there is no logical reason for doing so. And faith in your intuition will help lead you out of the rainstorm—if you learn to cultivate and follow it.

The good news is, if you don't have that kind of faith in yourself just yet, you can develop it (remember the affirmations tool?). You can develop it just by deciding to remind yourself every day that you are going to have faith in yourself, that you are going to find and feel and implement your internal guidance system, that you are going to practice patience, that you are going to practice trusting your instincts and believing that if you engage fully in the experiment of life, you will come to find your way out of the storm and into your blooming.

There were people who tried to tell me during the time of my brother's death that "everything happens for a reason." [Pro tip: that is a sentiment better left at the door when someone is struggling.] And though you may later come to recognize the gifts that evolved out of having faced your trauma, the trauma is still the trauma, and it is a lot to process. At some point, when you feel ready, begin to focus on the idea that who you are is the person who finds their way through the storm by being with it and seeking a path to the other side of it, even if it's on your hands and knees. You are the person whose soul can learn to rise no matter how long it takes. That's who you are. Don't forget it.

The Eightfold Path

Now, let's get clear on how to deal with the rainstorm, whatever that might be for you. Think of a place in your life when you have lost hope. It may be a tragedy you're dealing with and it may be a terrible numbing malaise with no direct cause that you understand yet. It may be an obstacle that you didn't deal with a long time ago that has now turned into a full-fledged storm, but whatever it is, it is hampering your ability to feel joyful and alive.

There is a concept in Buddhism called the Eightfold Path. It is usually presented something like this:

Right View
Right Purpose
Right Speech
Right Conduct
Right Livelihood
Right Effort
Right Awareness
Right Meditation

Got it? Me neither. These are simple words but very big concepts, and my understanding is truly introductory. But here's how my father—and I—break down these ideas (with the major disclaimer that neither of us are/were practicing Buddhists):

Right View
Bruce Lee (BL) Translation:
You must see clearly what is wrong.

Shannon Lee (SL) Translation: Know and understand what's wrong; see what the problem is. Feel your feelings and identify them: sadness, anger, disconnection, suffering. See where you are shut down or raging or hurt. Identify the source if you can.

Right Purpose
BL Translation: Decide to be cured.

SL Translation: Decide consciously that you don't wish to exist in this way anymore. Decide to do something about it. Decide to make a change and have full faith in the idea that you can live and be without this problem or live a full life within it.

Right Speech
BL Translation: Speak so as to aim at being cured.

SL Translation: Drop the doubt, the self-deprecation, the hedging of bets, the pretending, the lying. You are working on yourself—own it. Talk about the problem and the solution with optimism. Live in the possibility of your new way of being with the words that you speak.

Right Action

BL Translation: You must act.

SL Translation: Pull out your tools and get busy. Live your new way of being through your actions, through how you show up in the world. This doesn't mean you're perfect, but it means you are aiming for something and moving toward it. Read, take a class, go to therapy, do affirmations—take action!

Right Livelihood

*BL Translation: Your livelihood must
not conflict with your therapy.*

SL Translation: Don't engage in things that you know will derail you—bad habits, toxic environments, negative relationships. Your "therapy" is the actions you are taking and the words you are speaking as part of the new way of being you are creating for yourself. And your "livelihood" doesn't necessarily mean what you do for a living, but rather, your life, your aliveness, your environment. Don't knowingly throw obstacles into your path. Don't get in your own way. Don't let others stand in your way. Keep the path as clear as possible.

Right Effort

*BL Translation: The therapy must go forward
at the "staying speed."*

SL Translation: Like a marathon runner, if you come out of the gate too fast, you won't make it to the end. Don't be in a rush to "get there" like there's somewhere to get to. There is just life to live with as much aliveness and realness as possible for as long as possible. So move forward at a pace that you can sustain and fully embody.

Right Awareness
*BL Translation: You must feel it and
think about it incessantly.*

SL Translation: You have to want your cure. You have to keep your cure in mind and be aiming for it always. You don't need to be obsessed, but you have to be always for it. You don't want to forget about it. If you get off course, remember it and get back on course. You have to always keep it in the back of your mind, remain clear, and stay the course, again and again and again.

Right Meditation
*BL Translation: Learn how to contemplate
with the deep mind.*

SL Translation: The deep mind is the mind that listens to more than just itself. It is the mind that feels. It is the expansive mind. It is the mind integrated with the body and the soul. It is the mind that contemplates and doesn't just analyze. Engage the mind to try on your thoughts like an experience. Allow transformation from thought to feeling to being. Feel the possibility of expressing your thoughts through your actions so that the internal and the external can unite. Learn to engage the mind as an infinite, boundless creative cup to be filled over and over with your life force, which is then expressed through your being.

I know this is a lot, but don't get caught up too much in the order or the rules of this path. Just engage in the ecosystem. When I was in the rainstorm of my grief, I didn't have consciousness about my process for a good long while, and the thing that happened first for me was my incessant and desperate internal mantra of "Help me. I can't live like this anymore." I guess I could see clearly what was wrong in the sense that I knew I was in pain and grief. Then, when I found my father's words and immersed myself in them, I decided, unconsciously, to be cured and to act—because honestly, I couldn't live like that anymore. I started to follow whatever books and suggestions and possible paths came to me. None of this was methodical or purposeful, but I kept with it because my mental health depended on it. I moved at the staying speed as a matter of necessity.

And what followed was that I began to heal and life began to disclose itself to me. I began to move forward with clarity again. I decided after a time to take on the challenge of stewarding my father's legacy as a way of further embodying my therapy into my livelihood. It wasn't necessary for me to do that in order to be cured, but I felt called to it, and I have been blessed to be able to do it—even as more challenges arise as I continue to expand and grow and work to be myself. And I am only now beginning to fully appreciate and understand how to contemplate with the deep mind—what it means not just to think but to feel. That is some next-level stuff and it takes time. So be gentle and unrelenting; hold your own hand and keep pulling yourself forward. And if you have someone who will grab hold and pull you forward as well, then ask them for help, too.

All of this takes a level of sincerity and commitment. Remember how I said it wasn't necessarily going to be easy? But it also will get easier as it becomes a part of you and a way of life. It will transform you.

Enthusiasm Is God

My wish for you is to hold enthusiasm in your heart. Because enthusiasm is a natural by-product of conscious growth and healing. When
you see you have made it through the rainstorm, first you will sigh
with relief and then you will get excited. Fan that excitement like a
flame, and let it burn even brighter. My father said, "Enthusiasm is the
godhead within us and instinctively becomes the art of the physical becoming." When we are enthusiastic, we are inspired by life. We are in
joy; we are eager. If true confidence is lacking in you at the moment,
let curiosity give way to enthusiasm, for it will translate naturally into
a desire for engagement, a desire to play, and that desire will lead to
action and that action to aliveness and that aliveness to moments of
profound joy and confidence.

Remember the letter to Pearl my father wrote at twenty-one? In it
he also said, "I feel I have this great creative and spiritual force within
me that is greater than faith, greater than ambition, greater than confidence, greater than determination, greater than vision. It is all these
combined. My brain becomes magnetized with this dominating force,
which I hold in my hand."

Come to the realization that you hold a great creative and spiritual
force in your hand. That force is you. And you are yours to direct and
grow and create. That force is your potential waiting for discovery. It
is the light that will lead you out of the darkness.

I can honestly say, twenty-seven years after my brother's death, that
having delved deeply into the grief and healing of that trauma, I am a
better, more whole person today. I wish I could have learned the things
I learned without losing my brother; that will always be true, and I am
still learning so much now. But there were gifts that emerged through

the loss. Death is a serious teacher about life, about what it is to be alive, how impermanent everything is, how much there is to treasure, how little use there is for negativity and hate. These are lessons in the eternal qualities of the soul and resilience, lessons on true love and integrity, and lessons about letting go and acceptance. Lessons that led me here to you as I've traveled with the stream.

> There is nowhere for man to go out of this world; no tavern in which he can overcome anxiety; no jail in which he can expiate his guilt. So, instead of telling us what the problem is, Zen insists that the whole trouble is just our failure to realize that there is no problem. And, of course, this means that there is no solution either . . .

8

The Living Void

The void may be said to have two aspects:
It simply is what it is.
It is realized; it is aware of itself. And to speak improperly,
this awareness is "in us," or better, we are "in it."

In my father's water quote, there is a section about how water becomes the cup or the bottle or the teapot when put inside those forms. This is certainly a commentary on water's flexibility—that it quickly adapts to whatever situation it finds itself in. But it is also a commentary on what my father called the living void. It is the concept that water is in direct and immediate response and cocreation with its environment. It doesn't have to assess the cup and whether or not it will fit or how best to fill it. It just moves into place, naturally, immediately, and simply.

It Hits All by Itself

When the film *Enter the Dragon* was first released, there was a scene that my father had written and filmed that was cut out of the first part of the film initially. At the twenty-fifth anniversary, Warner Brothers put the full scene back in. In it my father is walking alongside a monk, who is his teacher, and the teacher is questioning him.

> Monk: *I see your talents have gone beyond the mere physical level. Your skills are now at the point of spiritual insight. I have several questions. What is the highest technique you hope to achieve?*
> Lee: *To have no technique.*
> Monk: *Very good. What are your thoughts when facing an opponent?*
> Lee: *There is no opponent.*
> Monk: *And why is that?*
> Lee: *Because the word I does not exist.*
> Monk: *So, continue.*
> Lee: *A good martial artist does not become tense, but ready. Not thinking, yet not dreaming. Ready for whatever may come. When the opponent expands, I contract. And when he contracts, I expand. And when there is an opportunity, I do not hit. It hits all by itself.*

"It hits all by itself." This is what it means to engage with the living void whether in martial arts or in life. But let's take a few steps back first and start with the beginning of what we know of the void.

It Simply Is What It Is

We have been speaking of emptiness as a state of mind up to this point—this idea of being open and present to what is happening without judgment or conditioned thinking. Remember choiceless awareness?

Emptying the cup of the mind? This is the first aspect of the living void. This first level of awareness is to release you from the prison of your inherently dualistic thoughts—good/bad, right/wrong—and to simply see things as they are without attachment. There is really nothing to try to do but accept, acknowledge, and sense everything that comes up moment to moment, including any resistance you may feel.

Another way of looking at this aspect of the void is to say the empty mind is the mental posture of honesty, sincerity, genuineness, and straightforwardness. In order to engage with what is happening openly, we have to be able to be fully honest and fully sincere with ourselves. We have to approach every experience head-on and without prejudice. If you can be fully present and honest about your experience, you can begin to truly research it. You will begin to notice what lights you up, what you love, as well as what turns you off and what you don't want. You begin to understand where the obstacles are—the people you stand in resistance to, the places where you lack attention, the patterns you repeat over and over. In this state, you get to understand and see what your obsessive thoughts are, your routines, your judgments, how you interact and react in relationships—but *if*, and only if, you can be directly honest and sincere with yourself.

> I mean it is easy for me to put on a show and be cocky
> and be flooded with a cocky feeling and then feel like
> pretty cool. . . . But to express oneself honestly, not
> lying to oneself . . . now that, my friend, is very hard
> to do.

Once we can stop lying to ourselves and get fully sincere, then all of the tools and ideas we have been talking about and practicing with up to this point have prepared us to be introduced to the living void.

I call it the "living void" because this is not some black hole of a void that swallows up everything in its path. This is a realm of heightened and effortless awareness, and it is very much alive. You are the active perceiver and feeler here, and you perceive without obstruction. My father had many names for the void: emptiness, nothingness, the formless form, etc. Another name my father used for this aspect of the living void is "no-mindedness." He said, "No-mindedness is not being without emotion or feeling but being one in whom feeling is not sticky or blocked—a non-graspiness of the mind." So we have an open mind and a sensing mind and an honest mind and now a mind that doesn't get hung up on anything. We are aware of our thoughts and feelings, but we do not get stuck in a feedback loop (obsessive, distracted, overwhelmed, confused).

> One can never be the master of his technical knowledge unless all his psychic hindrances are removed and he can keep the mind in the state of fluidity, ever purged of whatever technique he has obtained—with non-conscious effort.

When my father talks about "psychic hindrances," he is talking about anything that blocks your flow and your immediate expression. We want to remove these hindrances so we can move away from reaction and into skillful response.

In life, there are those who react and there are those who respond. A reaction is an unskilled expression, which happens when we are unaware of our state and our primal brain, or when our ego operates the machinery. A response is a skilled expression, in which our higher self is present and at the helm and we are making a natural and masterful choice.

So in order to remove our psychic hindrances, we have to be aware of them. We have to be aware of all our hang-ups and conditioning so that we can dissolve them. My father bids us to cultivate "a mind that has no dwelling place but continues to flow ceaselessly and moves beyond our limitations and our distinctions." We don't stop having distinctions or feeling limited; we just decide not to let them control us. We stay consciously aware in the ceaseless interplay of life. We remove our mental blocks, our obsessive thoughts, our calculating mind, our need to be better than, our need to look good in front of, and we just are—unapologetically, sincerely, honestly, fully ourselves.

From this masterful place, you no longer need to position yourself before you speak or act. You just speak or act with trust that you are being the most realized version of yourself in the moment of your action. All of our practicing is for this—a place where we no longer have to pause to analyze everything, where we no longer have to remember to pretend anything. As my father said, "The knowledge and skill you have achieved are, after all, meant to be 'forgotten' so you can float in emptiness comfortably, without obstruction." Imagine what it would be like to move confidently and naturally in every situation. It would be the ultimate in personal power, freedom, and expression. What does it take to achieve this level of personal proficiency?

The Stages of Cultivation

Now, you may think that there are a lot of people "not thinking" about what they do or what comes out of their mouths, and they don't seem like "masters of being" to you! And you would be right. There is unconscious behavior and there is conscious behavior. To address this progression from unconscious to conscious and then to the void, which is both conscious and unconscious, my father created his version of the stages of cultivation. For my father, there were four stages of cultivation, and they explained the process of maturity in human artistry for him.

In 1966, my father asked George Lee, who had made the miniature headstone for him, to also make him four plaques to represent the stages of cultivation he had determined for himself and his art of jeet kune do. The stages were:

Partiality
Fluidity
Emptiness
Jeet Kune Do

Stage One: Partiality

Partiality is where most of us start, and this is unconscious behavior. In martial arts, it's when you are a beginner and immature practitioner, and, to you, (by way of example) a punch is just a punch. Someone asks you to throw a punch; you've never thrown a punch before, so you just throw a punch. You don't think about how to do it best, and even if you kind of do, you think about it without any specific

knowledge on the subject—just what you think a punch should be like. It's a punch, but it's inelegant. There's an inexperienced, uncontrolled wildness to it; there's no technique, no skill. This stage is represented by a fragmented yin yang symbol with no inner relatedness and what my father called "the running to extreme."

When applying this stage to life, there's no awareness when it comes to thoughts, emotions, and actions. We are operating in unskilled reactions to what we narrowly perceive as good or bad, right or wrong. When we get defensive and are unwilling to listen and consider another's point of view or feelings, we are in partiality. We refuse to see that there is any other side, any other experience, or any other way. We refuse to give anyone the benefit of the doubt or take into consideration that they are coming from their own set of experiences and understanding of life up to this point. We refuse to see the blocks within ourselves that are keeping us trapped in behavioral patterns. We are being tossed around on the waves of life and we don't know where the shore is; we are just struggling to keep our heads above water at all costs.

Stage Two: Fluidity

Fluidity is the stage we reach once we've acknowledged that we (and everyone) have a lot to learn, and we begin to work on ourselves. It is the stage of a budding conscious awareness. In martial arts, this is where a punch is no longer just a punch. Suddenly we recognize all the intricacies that go into making a punch successful and we train and practice and start to gain skill. We begin to see that a punch doesn't just happen with the arm and fist, but that a good punch involves the whole body and the senses. We start to see that in order to punch well and find our target, we want to be in optimum condition, taking into consideration everything around us—who or what we are punching, where we are, how we feel, what's going on—and learn to work with

FLUIDITY
THE TWO HALVES OF ONE WHOLE

what is. My father called this the "two halves of one whole" and represented it on the plaque with a full yin yang symbol with two arrows encircling it, showing the constant interplay of the complementary forces.

In this stage, we are open and engaged in learning and bettering ourselves. We see that harnessing our potential is achievable, albeit both exciting and terrifying.

We acknowledge our mistakes and our blocks, and we create processes through which to practice, learn, and grow. We perceive that fluidity is a possibility, and balance and wholeness become real objectives because we are beginning to see the results of our awareness and our effort. We cultivate our tools, and we work to change ourselves and truly understand ourselves, which then starts to extend into our lives as compassion for everyone around us. Why compassion? Because as we start to grow and understand our own limitations, we begin to recognize and perceive the limitations that everyone experiences, and we feel for them in a new way.

I think my father dipped in and out of fluidity early on in his life, but I really liken this stage for him to the time after the fight in Oakland when he made a conscious effort to let go of his rigid training and look upon himself and his art with fresh eyes. In that pivot, he really started to tinker and express and reach. He began to deeply consider what it would take to be more whole as a martial artist and a human being. He worked for understanding and for skill as he delved into all manner of combat, fitness, nutrition, and philosophy. And he trained, discovered, and integrated it all into his life.

In fluidity, we see that life is rich and varied and that there is not only one solution to every problem. We engage our many tools and develop more. We become creative and more expressive. We begin to be able to have moments of flow and hunger to find consistency of flow. We learn how to accept the ever-changing nature of life and to work with rather than against it.

Stage Three: Emptiness

This is the stage of living void, or the "formless form," as my father memorialized it on his plaque within an empty black square.

This is where consciousness and unconsciousness begin to work together as one. There are no more halves, only wholeness. In our martial arts analogy, when we've reached stage three, the stage of emptiness, a punch is, once again, just a punch—meaning we have now gotten to a place of so much honed skill that we no longer have to think about how to punch or all the components of a punch or even

when to punch; now we can just punch. But this punch is a masterful punch—at once skillful and spontaneous.

My dear friend and colleague Chris gave me the novel *Musashi* by Eiji Yoshikawa, translated by Charles S. Terry. It's about real life seventeenth-century samurai Miyamoto Musashi, who wrote *The Book of Five Rings* (which my father had in his library), and I came across a passage in the novel that I think captures the living void beautifully:

> His plan came to him like a flash of light. It was not reasoned out by the theories of the Art of War, which constituted the fiber of the trained warrior's intuition. To reason out a mode of attack was a dilatory process, often resulting in defeat in situations where speed was of the essence. The warrior's instinct was not to be confused with animal instinct. Like a visceral reaction, it came from a combination of wisdom and discipline. It was an ultimate reasoning that went beyond reason, the ability to make the right move in a split second without going through the process of thinking.

Remember the scene from the opening of the chapter between Lee and the monk? The height of technique is to have no technique. Or, as in the Musashi quote, a course of immediate action is not to be reasoned out by theories or techniques on the art of war, but becomes the ability to make the right move in a split second without going through the process of thinking. The response just happens through a combination of wisdom and discipline that the warrior has attained. It emerges from the void, where there is no *I* and there is no opponent. There is only the totality of what is and what happens in response to what is. In other words, it hits all by itself! This is the ultimate in water level mastery.

In this stage of maturity, you are unlimited. You stand at the center point of possibility with the ability to move in any direction. This is no longer a tactical readiness but rather total awareness with instantaneous expression. Here, emptiness is not just a disciplined state of a mind free from judgment, but an environment for wise *and* instinctual creation where you cocreate your life fluidly and unstoppably with the moment. In this emptiness, we and the void are one.

In order to understand the process for achieving this advanced stage of emptiness (and before we can move on to stage four), we need to look a little more closely at the mechanics of getting there.

Bridging the Gap

In martial arts, there is a concept known as bridging the gap. The gap, most simply, is the space between you and your target or opponent. Whoever can bridge this gap most efficiently and effectively without getting caught in harm's way themselves is the one with the higher skill or the best kung fu. In martial arts, there are many tools you must have in your kit to do this well. You must have great mobility— quick footwork that can move in any direction. You must have a great sensitivity—being able to read your opponent and his movements by being fully present and responsive to the slightest changes in condition. You must have a great sense of timing—being able to find the perfect pockets of ingress that you can easily slip into. You must have great understanding—an ability to bring all your experience to bear. And you must have great spontaneity—being able to move at a moment's notice without telegraphing your movement ahead of time. It should be a seamless interplay of presence and movement. As my father said,

> In order to achieve oneness of movement and true flow,
> the gap between movements should be bridged.

But how do we apply this to life? What gap are we trying to bridge there? In martial arts, we are trying to bridge the gap that exists between us and our targets—and in life, that means everything that we interact with, such as our goals, our dreams, our relationships, and our work.

We want to bring the same martial arts tools to bear on our gap-bridging in life: we want to cultivate the skill of mobility—being able to come at a problem and move through life immediately and from a variety of angles. We want the skill of sensitivity—being able to sense what is called for in any situation by understanding what is happening and knowing how we feel and what we want. We want the skill of timing—being able not just to lead but to be led to the best moments for our impetus. We want the skill of understanding—having looked at and learned from our past experiences so that we can bring what wisdom we have attained to the situation. And we want the skill of spontaneity—being able to act in our best interest with full naturalness and immediacy, without being bogged down by too much thought.

Notice that the gap is the place of emptiness. It is, in truth, the birthplace of reality. It is the moment, however small, in which a choice is made. In this tiny gap lies the moment of decision, of action, of reflex, of thought. This empty gap is the place where consciousness and unconsciousness meet, for sometimes we make a conscious choice in that gap, and sometimes we react unconsciously, spurred on by our subconscious conditioning and our training. Oftentimes our choices are influenced by how much time we perceive we have to choose a path—a lot of time, and we can be more deliberate and conscious; no time, and we may act subconsciously. But the more we practice choosing quickly and the more we practice conditioning our subconscious, the smaller the gap becomes regardless of how much time we may be given. We learn to act from a place of cultivated instinct.

So imagine, if you will, that you can be in total concert with this gap, no matter how tiny. You could consciously choose your response with ease and confidence, or you could condition your subconscious mind with so much nutritious, positive practice that when you responded unconsciously, the response was still a perfect expression made with ease and confidence. What if this gap could become so tiny that it seemed to disappear altogether? That seamlessness is the feeling of true flow, where we are moving within the oneness.

As Bruce Lee reminds us . . .

> All movements come out of emptiness. The mind is the name given to this dynamic aspect of emptiness and emptiness is sincerity so there is no crookedness, no ego-centered motivation, only genuineness and straightforwardness which allows nothing between itself and its movements.

We want to practice bridging the gap between sensing and doing. I say "sensing" rather than "thinking" because traditionally, to think implies the analytical mind and does not include intuition, instinct, feeling, and the subconscious. Up to this point, we have been discussing how to develop the whole body as the sensing instrument to work in lockstep with the mind, and now we are looking at how to shorten the response time between sensing and doing, such that thought and action become the oneness of expression.

> What we are aiming for is for there to be no dislocation in the movements. They are done with flowing conti-

nuity like the movement of a river that is forever flowing without a moment of cessation or standing still.

How do we do this? Well, this is where the instruction manual
needs to be written by you. Through all of your practice and discovery, you will have started to develop a sense of what works best for
you. My father said "perception is the way of truth," but this is not
a perception that anyone can give to you. It is a perception that you
must uncover for yourself. It comes from effortless and pliable awareness upon which you can act immediately because you have done the
work to know yourself intimately—and because you are willing to
fully live and stand by your actions.

> Freedom is something that cannot be preconceived. To
> realize freedom requires an alert mind, a mind that is
> deep with energy, a mind that is capable of immediate
> perception without the process of graduation, with-
> out the idea of an end to be slowly achieved . . . At this
> point, many would ask, "how then do we gain this un-
> limited freedom?" I cannot tell you because it will then
> become an approach. Although I can tell you what it is
> not, I cannot tell you what it is. THAT, my friend, you
> will have to find out all by yourself!

This sense of freedom results from learning how to flow effort-
lessly in life. The effort we do apply is that of training, of working on
ourselves so that more and more, we can become more whole and
choose how we respond and participate in the rapid unfolding of life
with a growing sense of ease. We get to stop overthinking so much
and let naturalness become the norm. We've all had the experience
where we just knew what to do or what to say in a given moment, and

it felt so right and so natural, and there was an enthusiasm or easiness that permeated the whole exchange. It could be in a personal conversation or a pitch meeting or on the tennis court or in a fight, where you masterfully kept your cool because you could see the whole situation so clearly.

So how can we practice being one with the moment and bridging the gap? One way to look at it is in not second-guessing yourself once you've done a lot of good, solid personal practice. So, for example, when someone offers you a hand, you take it if that's what you instantly feel. Or when someone asks you to do something that doesn't feel right, you can simply say no, thank you. When someone offers you an opportunity (like sign this two-picture deal with an unproven new studio and producer in Hong Kong), you can sense immediately if it fits and you can say yes or no with full confidence.

It's Simple

The challenge with a notion such as the void is that it is at once simple to understand and difficult to implement. I love my father's description of simplicity. He said, "Simplicity is a quality of perception in approaching any problem." The void? Simple—be fully present, wise, and responsive in every moment. It's just so hard to actually do! The idea is fairly easily conveyed, but to gain this simplicity in the doing feels challenging and like it may take an inordinate amount of practice. To start, can you hold the idea of simplicity in your approach itself? It's true that you won't get it right all the time no matter how skilled you are. But we've let go of notions of right and wrong for ourselves. Mistakes are something for which we can be grateful, because there is no learning when we don't get things "wrong." And without learning, there is no expansion to the next level of being. So don't get bogged down in your approach before you practice; just simply practice.

When we break the idea of oneness into parts, we can become overwhelmed with all the different pieces—be observant while fully engaged, present while also sensing, responding naturally while also reaching for our dreams, knowing ourselves while also forgetting ourselves. Help! So instead I suggest that you don't break it into pieces—simply begin, and then practice and hone. And rather than trying to be more, aim to be less—less obstructed, less compartmentalized, less separate, with less ego. Over time, the less becomes more—more peaceful, more healthy, more whole, more real.

My father often likened the process of becoming one's true self to that of a sculptor. We are the chunk of raw marble, and rather than try to add more marble to make our sculpture, we are to chip away all that is hiding the art within. With every piece we chisel away, we reveal our true self. My father used this analogy with his martial arts as well:

> Being wise in gung fu does not mean adding more but
> being able to remove sophistication and ornamentation
> and be simply simple—like a sculptor building a statue
> not by adding, but by hacking away the unessential so
> that the truth will be revealed unobstructed.

"So that the truth will be revealed unobstructed"—this is what we are after. And to me, our "truth" equals our "soul." In my father's world, the height of cultivation means to move from being the experiencer (who can stand slightly to the side and evaluate the experience) to being the experience itself. When you are the experience itself, there is no time to assess ("this experience is great!")—there is only the experience, and it is what it is and we are it. This is being whole. This is oneness. This is true flow. And when we start flowing, some magical things start to happen. . . .

Magical Thing Number One: Your Pace Quickens

Many people who have come to see the archive of all my father's books and writings are astonished by the immense amount of output they encounter for a man who lived only to the age of thirty-two, during which time he also made movies, taught, and helped raise a family. And how was he able to be so prolific? By living in the void and not getting stuck in the gap without a bridge. And when you don't get stuck in the gap, your pace increases exponentially.

His pace of creation, of doing, was quick—not rushed, not harried and stressful, just immediate. He became so adept at translating thought into action (helped by his martial arts practice) that it became second nature to him. When he had an idea, he went immediately to the execution of that idea. Now, of course, not all ideas are good ideas, but you get to the good ones faster if you move through the bad ones faster. The goal isn't *not* to fail; the goal is to fail faster so that the lessons from the failures can be implemented and lead you to success more quickly.

How many of us have stuff we want to do, but we put it off over and over? Think about whenever you've had a thought, even one such as "I need to do the dishes," but then you didn't act on it. And later you beat yourself up for still not having done the dishes, or maybe you have the thought five more times before you actually get up and do them, and then while you're doing them, you're kind of annoyed by having to do them because now you've left them until you're tired and you just want to go to bed. Now think about having the thought that you need to do the dishes and then just doing them. Done. Boom. Next. No time wasted on extra thoughts about it or berating yourself over it—the task (and yourself) no longer imbued with negativity that bogs you down.

Now use this example for something bigger. You have the thought, "I've always wanted to write a novel." And when you have that thought, you are filled with wonder and enthusiasm. Now, if that thought is followed by further thoughts about your potential inadequacy or how you don't have time or how ridiculous the idea is (after all, you're not a writer), you're in the gap without so much as a rickety suspension bridge. But if you instead follow that thought with grabbing a pen or opening your computer to start putting down your ideas, or signing up for an online course on how to write a novel, you're no longer in the gap. You've moved across it. And whether you write a whole novel or not, you now have the start of something to play with. And you now get to decide how much of your effort you want to put toward the full execution of it. It may ultimately take you ten years to actually write a novel. But guess what: if you fall into the gap between thought and action (the black hole version of the void, rather than the living, cocreating kind), and you never get started, all you'll have in ten years is a lot of wasted time and energy on thoughts and feelings about the novel you never wrote and no novel to show for it.

Let's look at a different example. You are in a conversation with someone you've just gotten to know recently, and you have the thought, "I really like this person; I feel so good when I'm with (him/her/them)," but you second-guess yourself and you don't express it. Now this person never knows how you feel about them; you miss an opportunity to bring your relationship closer by fostering some potential connection with them; and you've sacrificed your own self-expression in the moment. Or should I say, in the gap. That's not to say every thought needs to be expressed, but when it feels like an expression of your soul, then practice honestly expressing yourself out loud, in real time.

How do you know what is an expression of your soul? Well, first, don't take it from me—experiment and figure it out (go back to earlier chapters). Play with expressing and not expressing and see what feels right. If you don't express something, and it keeps popping into your mind unbidden, then it is likely looking for expression, and you get to decide what the appropriate expression is. Notice how your body feels. When you feel light, energized, and uplifted, you should follow that. When your body feels constricted, sinking, or depleted, figure out how to expiate, express, and expel this feeling in a productive way. But don't get caught up in the gap of either a missed opportunity or stewing. Learn to move into positive, unrestricted action, and you will suddenly accomplish so much more in much less time—and you will look back and be amazed by your progress.

Magical Thing Number Two:
You Feel Powerful

Another magical thing that can happen when bridging the gap and living in the void is personal empowerment. You begin to feel like the master of your own destiny. You are captaining the ship. Your insides are starting to match your outsides—meaning, you are aligning your thoughts and your actions. You are becoming your real and fully responsive self in every instance. You no longer have to wear a carefully constructed mask for anyone or hide who you really are. That feels good and allows you to feel more confident and ultimately more empowered.

This can be a little scary at first, but when you clean out your mental closet and take responsibility for your thoughts and actions, there's a maturing that happens. It's called being authentic.

> One is the captain of one's soul, the master of one's life. What causes such realization and subsequently causes a shift in one's behavior? To be real. To accept responsibility for oneself.

There's an e. e. cummings quote that I love that says: "It takes courage to grow up and be who you really are." And it's true. To become fully expressive and responsible for all one's actions and choices is some serious adulting. But if there's one thing I have noticed time and time again, it's that no matter the situation, people deeply appreciate it when others are authentic and take responsibility for themselves, especially if they can do so with kindness. And it's not only good for the recipient; it's good for the responsible party as well. Yes, it can be hard and even painful, too, but it builds integrity. And having integrity leads to a sense of empowerment and wholeness.

What might it look like to be responsible and clear in your communications? What would it be like to release yourself from codependence and stand on your own sturdy feet? Can you be caring *and* honest? Can you be truthful *and* loving? How powerful would it feel to speak and act with immediacy from your heart with confidence and compassion?

My father said, "Every circumstance of every man's life is the result of a definite cause—mode and control are yours." Mode and control are yours. You have the ability to own your circumstances, to truly see yourself and then to be in conscious collaboration with yourself and your life, and you get to decide how to do that. There's no right way or wrong way; there's only taking responsibility or not. And taking responsibility is empowering. It gets less scary the more you practice it, and the more natural it becomes, the closer you are to living in the void. The closer you are to functioning from the root of your being.

> The root is the fulcrum on which will rest the expression of your soul; the root is the "starting point" of all natural manifestation. It cannot be, when the root is neglected, that what should spring from it will be well-ordered.

From a well-ordered and rooted soul springs a grounded and authentic life. And when you live up to your heart and soul's authenticity, you do so humbly and without needing validation because you know who you are. You don't need anyone else to give that to you. You can be authentic and creative within the living void, leaping confidently over all the gaps, simply because it makes you feel powerfully whole to do so.

Magical Thing Number Three: You Are Safe!

When you're living in the void and you feel whole and authentic and you are flowing, you start to feel safe. When I say safe, I mean internally safe—feeling like you can trust yourself, take care of yourself, stand up for yourself, be okay no matter who you're with or what's happening, and be yourself without fear. When your efforts become natural and purposeful, you don't have to prove a point or position yourself or manipulate a situation or a relationship to be sure others think well of you. You may think that you do that stuff because it feels good and powerful and you're being clever, but mostly you do it because you don't feel good enough or powerful enough just as you are; and when you don't feel good enough or powerful enough, you're likely to feel unsure and inadequate and fearful—you feel unsafe.

That feeling of insecurity is a powerful driver to do whatever we can to make it go away. But the true warrior (meaning the regular person who tackles life head-on) doesn't look for safety from the outside. They work to nurture their own sense of internal security, which comes from working diligently to know themselves and make an ally out of change and the unknown. If you have the mental image of a warrior as someone who runs out bravely and determinedly into battle, translate that image instead into the image of someone who valiantly takes on whatever life throws at them with grace and determination, someone who doesn't turn away from a challenge or from acknowledging their own shortcomings, someone who doesn't seek just an ideal image but rather an ideal soul. That's a modern-day warrior and a hero.

And, by the way, warriors also feel fear, but what they don't typically feel is insecure or unsafe. They don't feel unsafe because they know they have the tools and the skills and the confidence to solve their own problems or to meet failure with grace; they know they are in cocreation with their life and all the lives around them. *They* choose when to act and when to stand down. They are deeply in touch with their abilities, and so they can move swiftly over the gap and move definitively within the void to take action in the face of a beautiful flowing stream or a raging storm, whatever it is that shows up.

> Let's just put it this way: I have no fear of an opponent in front of me; I am very self-sufficient. They do not bother me. And then, should I fight, should I do anything, I have made up my mind, and that's it, baby . . .

And that leads us, my friends, to stage four. . . .

9

The Way of the Intercepting Fist

Using no way as way,
having no limitation as limitation.

Stage Four: Jeet Kune Do

The final stage of cultivation for my father was his art of jeet kune do. In our martial arts analogy, this is where a punch is not only a highly skilled yet natural punch as in stage three, but it is entirely your own. It is imbued with your own very real and very unique expression. There will never be another Bruce Lee, and this fourth stage in the progression is why—it requires us to be the quintessential version of ourselves. Only Bruce Lee could be his fourth stage, and only you can be yours.

Bruce Lee was so quintessentially himself that no one else will ever come close to truly imitating him. The way he moved, the sounds he made, the way he spoke, his handwriting, his musculature, it was all artisanal—crafted by his own hand and through his own effort. He didn't seek to create himself in anyone else's image. He sought only to be himself. And that he did magnificently. I think this is the thing we sense in him when we see him—that he is somehow this heightened version of what is possible in a human being, and it feels extraordinary and exciting.

My father's final, fourth stage was so much more than a name for a martial arts system to him. In fact, he recoiled at the notion of calling it a system or a style at all, because those words tend to separate and limit people and artistry. He even went so far as to suggest that if people get too caught up in the name "jeet kune do," arguing over what it is and what it isn't, that it is better that it disappear altogether, as it was never meant to confine or separate the practitioners. Rather, jeet kune do is the direct expression of Bruce Lee. It is a reflection of his soul made visible. This was as close to the concretization and physicality of his essence on earth as he could get. It most definitely reflected his expression of the martial arts, but it also encompassed his expression of life. As he said, everything he had learned about life, he learned through his martial arts.

Jeet kune do translates to "the way of the intercepting fist," and if you have been paying attention, then you may be starting to see why this is the perfect expression of all we have been discussing. To me, this name beautifully and simply reveals the idea of bridging the gap. The fist doesn't just hit; it intercepts. It responds. It is in relationship to what is. It is alive, ushered forth out of the void and into direct correlation with reality.

The fourth and final plaque my father created to represent this wholly personal and realized stage had the yin yang symbol with the arrows around it as in the fluidity stage, but with his personal maxim in Chinese characters encircling it as well, which translate to: "Using no way as way, having no limitation as limitation." The very essence of water—ever finding its own path without limit.

You may wonder why his fourth stage has so much form to the design of the plaque when it may seem like emptiness, the formless form, is the ultimate goal. Remember that the living void is the emptiness from which all our personal expression springs forth. Yes, an understanding of it and a collaboration with it is essential, but we are the secret ingredient that makes the void live through us. We are the unique and alive expression in this human realm.

So this fourth stage of cultivation is all you—you as the expression of your life, of your heart, of your soul. If you were to consider what that might be, what do you come up with? For myself, I would have to be honest and say that I don't totally yet know. I'm a late bloomer. But I hold space for it to become clearer to me, and in the meantime I hold on to the things I know are clear already, and I practice bringing them from the inside out with more and more skill each passing day. This is the process. My father has a quote about enlightenment that speaks to this:

> To obtain enlightenment, emphasis should fall NOT on
> the cultivation of a particular department which then
> merges into the totality, but rather, on the totality that
> then enters into and unites the particular departments.

To me this means that to obtain wholeness and full personal potential, we need to work not from the outside in, but from the inside out. We don't need to spend all our time making the external stuff of our lives look a certain way so that we can then be joyful and peaceful and powerful. Instead we should work on being joyful, peaceful, and powerful and then bring that through into all the things we do and want and manifest in our lives. In other words, don't put all your focus and energy into your career so that one day you will be content and happy. Work on being content and happy and bring that into your career and the rest of your life.

In this way, our lives become a true reflection of who we really are without artifice. And in this way, when we go to act, we do not have to wrestle with ourselves to know what to do. We are already sure of what's important and what we want, and we are committed to it no matter what.

So how did Bruce Lee show his commitment to what was important to him?

Enter the Motherf***ing Dragon

One of my father's students was Ted Ashley, the head of Warner Brothers studio at the time. Warner Brothers had tried to get a TV series starring my father off the ground (that series, *Kung Fu*, was ultimately made starring a white actor playing a Chinese man), and they

had also put some development interest behind a project my father
had created with writer (and student) Stirling Silliphant called *The Silent Flute,* for my father and James Coburn to star in, to no avail. But
now that my father had left Hollywood for a detour through Hong
Kong and was smashing all the box office records one film after another, his supporters at Warner Brothers finally had the proof they
needed to sell the studio on doing a film with Bruce Lee.

Enter the Dragon was the dream opportunity coming true for my
father—a Hollywood feature for him to star in. That said, Hollywood
billed it as a double lead in case their gamble on my father didn't pay
off, and in part due to the intense prejudice and concern surrounding
the xenophobia of audiences of that time. But my father didn't worry
himself with this. He knew he had the goods even if others weren't
sure. He was ready to make the absolute most of this opportunity
to accomplish his goal of showing the Western world the glory of
Chinese gung fu and to express himself fully in a true, on-screen representation of a Chinese man.

There was only one problem. The script was terrible. So terrible,
in fact, that my father was adamant that the writer be fired and sent
back to California while he himself feverishly rewrote the majority of
the screenplay. Of course, the studio didn't listen to my father and kept
the writer in Hong Kong, making small tweaks to this actioner that
was initially entitled *Blood and Steel* and later the inventive *Han's Island*
(while lying to my father and telling him they had sent him back to Los
Angeles). This original script had none of the iconic scenes that exist
today. No "finger pointing at the moon." No "art of fighting without
fighting." No philosophical scene with the monk discussing the true
nature of mastery—"*I* do not hit. It hits all by itself."

It was of utmost importance to my father that this film reflect his
art and culture accurately and with depth. This was his moment to
show the world who he was and what a Chinese gung fu man could

do, and he was not going to settle for mediocre. So he rewrote the script and submitted his rewrites to the producers. He also argued back and forth with the studio over the title. His Chinese stage name was Siu Loong, which translates to "Little Dragon," and this film was to be his introduction to the West. The title *Enter the Dragon* had a power and a specificity that *Han's Island* and *Blood and Steel* did not. He wrote numerous letters to Warner Brothers petitioning for this name change: "Do consider carefully the title 'Enter the Dragon.' I really think this is a good title because *Enter the Dragon* suggests the emergence of someone that is quality." That "quality someone" he is referring to is, of course, himself!

The studio finally succumbed to this request and agreed to rename the film. My father trained like he had never trained before and worked continuously on the script to make it as good as possible. His production company, Concord Productions, became the Hong Kong production entity to make the film (though my father is not credited as a producer), and he was also tapped with choreographing the entire movie. He worked night and day to make the most of this opportunity he had been given. He was going to show Bruce Lee to the world.

As he wrote in a letter to Ted Ashley:

> I am sure you agree with me that quality, extreme hard work, and professionalism is what cinema is all about. My twenty years of experience, both in martial arts and acting has led to the successful harmony of showmanship and genuine, efficient, artful expression. In short, this is it, and ain't nobody knows it like I know it. Pardon my bluntness, but that is me! You see, my obsession is to make, pardon the expression, the fuckingest action motion picture that has ever been made. In closing, I will give you my heart, but please do not give me your

head only. In return, I, Bruce Lee, will always feel the deepest appreciation for the intensity of your involvement.

The first day of shooting finally arrived, and the Hong Kong crew and the American crew were there and poised to begin, with various translators on set to help the two crews communicate with each other. My father, however, was a no-show—he refused to come to set. You see, the final locked shooting script had been issued, and it did not incorporate the pages he had written. None of his changes had been made.

One could argue that, in this moment, my father should have just done this movie as they wanted it, and then hoped it did well enough to get him the next opportunity, where maybe he could have had more creative control—a way to get his foot in the door and try to inch it open further and further with each subsequent project. But my father had already tried this in Hollywood, and he knew it didn't work. He knew that if he didn't take a stand, he would be marginalized over and over again by people who "knew better."

And so the standoff began.

The crew started filming what shots they could that did not involve my father, and my father stayed in our house and refused to come to set until the changes were made. The producers would come to the house to try to reason with him. They would talk to my mom, who would act as the go-between when my father was fed up and refused to entertain any more of their rationalities about why they couldn't do what he wanted. And my father continued to put his foot down. He told them they had the script for the movie he wanted to make, and if they used that script, he would happily show up to set.

The producers created cover-up stories about how my father was so nervous about being in a Hollywood movie and being a failure that he was terrified to show up to set. In books that were written many years after my father died, Fred Weintraub spun this tale of paralyzing fear on the part of my father—to the utter disgust and dismay of my mother and my family. Bruce Lee was not afraid of this opportunity. In fact, he was the only person who recognized the full nature of the opportunity and what it could be, and he would have rather blown it up than wasted it by doing something half-assed. He knew he would only get one chance to be introduced to the world. My mom urged the producers and director to pay attention, telling them, "He knows what he's talking about. You should listen to him."

The standoff continued for two weeks. As time went on, the crew ran out of shots to grab without their star and choreographer, and ended up sitting around with nothing to do at a substantial cost to the studio. Tensions were running high among the cast and crew. The producers began to get pressure from Warner Brothers to get the production back on track, and there was only one way that was going to happen.

The producers finally gave in to my father's demands. They implemented the script changes he had made and agreed to shoot the film he envisioned.

When I asked my mom years later if he had really been willing to lose the opportunity rather than submit to their demands, she said without hesitation, "You bet!" Bruce Lee had taken a stand and held to his core. He brought the full force of his expression and his being into play because he knew what was important to his soul. He had stayed true to his center and in so doing, the full force of the tornado that was him changed the landscape around him forever.

Enter the Dragon became a global phenomenon and cemented my father as an icon of martial arts and culture.

In My Own Process

Interestingly, thanks to my father's diligent writing process, we actually know what was running through his mind a month or two before he started filming his final movie. At the start of 1973, my father was enmeshed in filming his movie *Game of Death* while at the same time finishing up negotiations to appear in the Hollywood feature he had been seeking for many years. He would have to put *Game of Death* on hold to pursue his dream of the East-meets-West Hollywood actioner, which ultimately became *Enter the Dragon*.

It was at this moment, during a time of his life that could not have been more busy, anticipatory, and important (and which also happened to be shortly before the end of his life), that my father attempted to pen an article, which he called "In My Own Process." The article was never finished. Instead what we have are several handwritten drafts that seem like a manifesto of sorts. He declares his identity, and he seems to be aching to express in writing some essential truths that he has come to know—about himself and about life.

> I am in the midst of preparing my next movie *Enter the Dragon*, a production between Concord and Warner Bros., plus another Concord production, *The Game of Death*, which is only halfway done. I have been busy and occupied with mixed emotions of late.

He seemed to need to get something off his chest. Maybe it was a result of energy begetting energy. When things are amped up and busy, energy seems to expand and even more creative expression can yearn to be manifested or conveyed. Or maybe he had a cosmic sense that time was running out. Or maybe it was just a natural part of his way of being. In any case, he was a man on the verge of realizing a big dream and feeling a need to center and express himself.

Another striking thing about these drafts is that they are somewhat fevered, marked by a great many cross-outs and inserts. They are actually hard to read. The usually beautiful penmanship is sacrificed here in service to an urgency to say something vital.

> What it boils down to is my sincere and honest revelation of a man called Bruce Lee . . . Just who is Bruce Lee? Where is he heading? What does he hope to discover? . . . Oh I know I am not called upon to write any true confession, but I do want to be honest—that is the least a human being can do. Basically, I have always

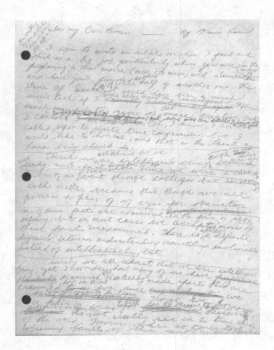

been a martial artist by choice and an actor by profession. But, above all, I am hoping to actualize myself to be an artist of life along the way.

These drafts are rich with insight and desire, but I bring them up because they also served, at a very crucial point in his life, as a very timely reminder and grounding device. He seems to be prompting himself to remember who he is, what he wants, and what is important so that he could hold true to himself, the root of his being, in the moments that were to come. "Above all," he said, "I am hoping to actualize myself to be an artist of life." *Above all.*

This is what our journey is leading toward: the understanding that the greatest possible expression we can have, and the greatest growth and impact, stems from the very root of our being. Stage four. When we are rooted, when we have absolute faith and trust in our purpose and ourselves, then we are free. Free to choose. Free to create. Free to make a stand. Free to be—no matter the circumstances or the situation. And though this may not come easily, when we directly choose to undertake difficulty, it is in order to be free.

Enter the Dragon is a feat of filmmaking not because it's a great piece of cinema. The plot is pretty unremarkable and predictable and the seventies kitsch is in full effect (though the kitsch is pretty great!). Enter the Dragon is iconic because Bruce Lee got to be Bruce Lee in it and to realize his vision in a vehicle that had the capacity to travel around the world. In the "In My Own Process" drafts just a few months before, my father said, "I am happy because I am growing daily and honestly, and I don't know where my ultimate limit lies. To be certain, every day there can be a revelation or a new discovery that I can obtain. However, the most gratification is yet to come; to hear another human being say, 'Hey, now here is someone real.'"

And when you watch Enter the Dragon, that is what you see. It is the experience of seeing a self-actualized, self-expressed, confident, lights-turned-all-the-way-on human being beaming off the screen and into your imagination. Suddenly the possibility of what a person can be becomes real, and it is mesmerizing. Kung fu flick aside, watching Bruce Lee is like watching a real-life dragon fly.

How Can I Be Me?

This may seem like a paradox, but to be able to fly, truly free and expressed, you need to be truly rooted and grounded. Remember, my father said, "The root is the fulcrum on which will rest the expression of your soul; the root is the 'starting point' of all natural manifestation.

It cannot be, when the root is neglected, that what should spring from it will be well-ordered."

All this talk about knowing yourself and practicing and developing your skills is to get you to the place of understanding and realizing your potential, to get you to the place where you know both when it's time to make your stand and hold your ground with purpose and without malice, *and* when it's time to yield your will to the natural unfolding of things and follow or move on. The root of who you are is the essential ingredient to your specific unfolding. Without you, there is no direction for your flow. You must practice to gain this—and what you gain is nothing less than yourself.

My father said, "When I look around, I always learn something and that is to be always yourself, and to express yourself, to have faith in yourself. Do not go out and look for a successful personality and duplicate it. Start from the very root of your being, which is 'how can I be me?'" He believed that this achieving center, being grounded in oneself, was about the highest state a human being could achieve.

And it is from this place of grounding and knowing and embodying that we can stand in our confidence, our doing, our strength, and our calm like the eye of a powerful storm that we get to direct.

> We are vortices whose center is a point that is motionless and eternal but which appears as motion that increases in velocity in the manner of a whirlpool or tornado (whose epicenter is still). The nucleus is in reality whereas the vortex is phenomenon in the form of a multidimensional force field. HOLD TO THE CORE!!!

It was this sentiment that led my father to stand his ground and risk it all for the integrity of his being in 1973.

Being wholly ourselves is freedom—not being under the control or power of anyone else mentally, emotionally, spiritually, but rather, personally permitted to act on behalf of ourselves. If you are afraid you will lose too much in this undertaking, then consider it a loss of all that is not you to the gain of all that is. And the only way to find out if what I'm saying is true is to try it on for yourself.

The Moon in the Stream

We have spoken a lot now about being powerful, fully expressed, and free, but I'd like to give you one more benefit to consider about our water journey. I'd like to make a case for the idea that the deepest root of all of this glorious personal unfolding is a deep peacefulness. Remember my father's "Definite Chief Aim" (from chapter five), where he lays out his goal to be a successful actor and martial artist? Well, at the end of that document he says that the aim of all that achieving is to live in inner harmony and happiness. This inner peace is the true depth of power.

Remember that, in the void, from which springs everything, resides nothing. It is emptiness, space. It is stillness. Where is the hurricane its most calm? At its center. As my father said, "The real stillness is stillness in movement." To me, this means that when we know ourselves and accept ourselves, we have attained a certain peace with ourselves. We harbor no qualms; we are being real. There is peace to that security, and the authentic power we generate stems from this. We are able to act and encounter the unknowns of life from this place of absoluteness, from the vast quiet and infinity of space.

Think about it. How much does it take to face a challenge with calm and grace? It's easy to fly off the handle and get riled up and combative. But when you can stand ready to face an opponent (or face yourself) and feel prepared for whatever may come, that requires a certain quiet strength. This is an immovable peacefulness, a deep stillness, a powerful knowing.

I like to visualize a small but brilliant spiral galaxy surrounded by the star-studded blackness of space at the center of my solar plexus. It helps me to remember that the void is part of me and that I have access to the infinite. Whenever I feel limited or overly reactionary, I just try to tap back into that tiny vastness at the center of my will and remind myself that, whatever my outward circumstance, I am not trapped inwardly. I am, in fact, boundless.

My father called this being "the moon in the stream." Picture a full moon shining down and reflected in a running stream. The stream is in motion all the time, but the moon retains its serenity even as the waters flow and churn.

> The waters are in motion all the time, but the moon
> retains its serenity. The mind moves in response to the
> ten thousand situations but remains ever the same.

The Secret to Nirvana

My father loved the goddess Kwan Yin. We had more than one representation of her in our house—a big stone head of the goddess that resided in the garden and a full, life-size wooden carving of her seated with one leg casually bent at an angle over the other in the posture of repose.

When I was a little girl in Hong Kong, I used to sit in the lap of the goddess. She had the perfect-size lap for my toddler body. She felt to me like a place of refuge, this goddess of compassion and mercy. She holds a special place in my heart still. In Eastern religions she is one goddess who permeates across multiple cultures. She is celebrated in India, China, Japan, Korea, and Southeast Asia, and perhaps many other places as well. She is oftentimes associated with the qualities of the Western world's Mother Mary.

My father liked to use Kwan Yin as an example of the fluid mind or the moon in the stream—free to move with the stream while also retaining its serenity and wholeness. He illustrates this with his portrait of the goddess below.

> Kwan Yin, the goddess of Mercy, is sometimes represented with one thousand arms, each holding a different instrument. If her mind stops with the use, for instance, of a spear, all the other arms (999) will be of no use whatsoever. It is only because of her mind not stopping with the use of one arm, but moving from one instrument to the other, that all her arms prove useful with the utmost degree of efficiency. Thus the figure is meant to demonstrate that, when the ultimate truth is realized, even as many as one thousand arms on one body may each be serviceable in one way or another.

The idea then is that this unperturbed freedom we've been discussing is a character of mind that we need to possess—a mind endowed with infinite mobility. It can think anything, dream anything, believe anything, imagine anything, see anything, inspire anything, hold anything. Fluidity of mind is a mind that can direct as many as one thousand arms but does not get in the way of any of it—the mind follows its course like the many currents in the stream. Our practice is in taking everything in and not allowing our attention to be arrested. The mind does not stop at one object that is perceived, but rather perceives all.

> Moving and yet not moving, in tension and yet relaxed, seeing everything that is going on and yet not at all anxious about the way it may turn, with nothing purposely designed, nothing consciously calculated, no anticipation, no expectation—in short, standing innocently like a baby and yet with all the cunning of the keenest intelligence of a fully matured mind.

My father said that the delusive mind (the mind that misleads itself) is the mind intellectually and effectively burdened (too clever for its own good). It cannot move on from one moment to another without reflecting on itself, and this obstructs its native fluidity and therefore its creativity, its authentic expression, and its freedom. A wheel cannot revolve when it is too tightly attached to the axle. When the mind is tied up, the focus too narrow or obsessed, it feels inhibited in every move it makes (like trudging through the stickiest mud), and nothing will be accomplished with any sense of spontaneity.

"Spontaneity" may seem frivolous, like deciding to jump in the pool with your clothes on, or even irresponsible, like dropping everything and flying off to Cancún on a whim. But my father held spontaneity sacred because, to him, it reflected a state where inspiration is mixed with instinct and the confidence to execute this immediate calling in the moment of its occurrence. Spontaneity was real magic that could usher through him like a flash of lightning, or like a punch that catches your opponent before he can even make a move.

I am reminded of the scene in *Enter the Dragon* where Lee squares off with one of the villains, named O'Hara, at the tournament. They set hands to prepare to fight, and before O'Hara even knows what's happening, Lee has struck him and he's down on the ground. It is one immediate movement. It is intuited spontaneity of the most effective order, and it was so lightning fast that in reality, it was hard to even catch on film.

> To be consciously unconscious or to be unconsciously
> conscious is the secret to nirvana. The act is so direct
> and immediate that no intellection finds room to insert
> itself and cut it to pieces.

Why is this the secret to nirvana? Because all the doubt, second-guessing, worry, analysis, judging, neediness, mask-wearing, and perfectionism that takes so much of our energy doesn't exist here. Everything is immediate in this active emptiness, and it springs from the total sincerity of who we are. When we train to know ourselves, then we gain assuredness and confidence. In becoming our quintessential selves, we reach our fourth stage of cultivation, which feels phenomenal. Perhaps it even feels like nirvana.

Think about when you've ever had a terrible pain, like a toothache or a migraine, or maybe even a bad cough that went on for weeks. Remember when it went away, and your whole body could just relax? Your shoulders stopped being hunched up by your ears, you felt like you could breathe, your jaw and your intestines stopped gripping. You had clarity, you could focus. This is the same feeling of living in your truth. Relaxed yet strong. Peaceful yet enthusiastic. Ready to meet (or intercept!) every moment as it unfolds no matter what it may bring your way. Sounds like nirvana to me.

> Recognize and use the spiritual power of the infinite.
> The intangible represents the real power of the universe.
> It is the seed of the tangible. It is living void because all
> forms come out of it, and whosoever realizes the void is
> filled with life and power and the love of all beings.

What Is Essentially Your Own

Remember when my father said in the letter to Pearl in 1962 that he could feel this great power inside him? Hold that thought—because this power, this creative tide, also exists within you, and it is yours for the using.

Now take a moment to really feel that power. Close your eyes (or don't) and sit and breathe, and instead of concentrating, consciously loosen. Spread your perception throughout your whole body. What can you feel? Can you feel the aliveness and energy inside your whole being? Can you feel yourself expand? Can you feel the life-giving force that animates your cells? Can you feel that this essence radiates through and exists for you to use?

This is your essence. This is your untapped power that you hold in the palm of your hand. And the stoking and freeing of this essence is what we are after.

> When man comes to a conscious realization of those great spiritual forces within himself and begins to use those forces in life, his progress in the future will be un-paralleled. To raise our potential is to live every second refreshed. Trust the life-giving force within.

Remember what my father said in the "In My Own Process" drafts? He wanted above all to be an "artist of life." An artist is a creator. He takes raw materials, takes his environment, and creates something that comes from within his soul. An artist of life creates his own life, creates himself, moment by moment. And in his ability to choose and create, he is powerful and free.

Remember that my father's recipe when it came to his art of jeet kune do was to research your own experience, reject what is useless, accept what is useful, and "add what is essentially your own."

> To live is to express oneself freely in creation. Creation, I must say, is not a fixed something. At best, Bruce Lee presents a possible direction, and nothing more. You are free to make your own choice and express your instinctive potentiality. I am actualizing myself daily to be an artist of life! In life, what can you ask for but to fulfill your potential and be real!

10

My Friend

Do you know how I like to think of myself? As a human being.
Because under the sky, under the heavens, there is but one family.

Bruce Lee Remembered

My father died on July 20, 1973, of a cerebral edema—a swelling of
the brain. The autopsy report determined that it had occurred as a
result of an allergic reaction to a pain medication he had been given
for a headache. Many theories have circulated about the cause of his
death, from the fantastic (he was killed by ninjas or by the mysterious
death touch or by gang lords) to the medical (he died from an allergy
or a specific form of epilepsy or heat exhaustion). I can accept that we
may never know exactly how he died. To focus on his death rather
than his life is to focus on the finger and not the moon, and is, to me,
the true loss.

When my father passed away, there was a huge public funeral

in Hong Kong. But he was not ultimately buried there. Rather, my mother decided to bring him back to Seattle (the town where they had met and fallen in love) to be laid to rest. It was a controversial decision for the people of Hong Kong, who considered Bruce Lee to be their native son, but for my mother, it was a matter of keeping her children's father close to them and returning him to a place where he had known great peace, simplicity, and inspiration.

My father always talked about his professional time in Hong Kong as temporary. The idea was to ultimately live and work predominantly in California, but my mother and father often reminisced about retiring one day, in their golden years, to Seattle, a place they both had a great fondness for. And so, when he passed, my mother brought my father to Seattle to lay him to rest.

There was a small, private ceremony for close friends and family at Lake View Cemetery overlooking Lake Washington in Seattle, where many of my father's first ideas and first loves began. It is as beautiful and picturesque a cemetery as I have seen. And there he remains to this day.

When it came time to create his headstone, a challenging task under any circumstance, much thought and discussion went into it. It was decided that his headstone would have a photo of him on it with all the pertinent, identifying information of his life and death, while at the bottom, parallel with the ground, a platform would hold an open stone book. On one side of the page, the book would bear my father's core symbol (from stage four)—the yin yang with arrows around it and the Chinese phrase "Using no way as way, having no limitation as limitation." And on the other side would read the words, "Your inspiration continues to guide us toward our personal liberation."

You see, back then, in 1973, the people who knew Bruce Lee best knew full well that he was a phenomenal thinker and doer, and they

understood that there was much to integrate for themselves through the example of his words and actions. They appreciated fully his genuineness and his aliveness. They absorbed so much from just having spent time with him, learning from him, and being with him. His energy and integrity were palpable, revelatory, and moving. I recently came across a quote that I thought was very applicable to my father's life. It read, "True mastery is service." What that means to me is that the energy imparted and expressed through someone's mastery is in and of itself an act of service because it lifts us up and inspires us to what is possible in life. You shine your own light, and there's more light, in total, for everyone.

He inspired, if not overwhelmed, anyone who came into contact with him. And he was the model of what it is to be fully creative and expressive, authentically powerful, and personally liberated. He was not bound like we tend to bind ourselves. You could see it, feel it, hear it, and know it. And it's not to say he was perfect (he most certainly was a human being like you and me), but he was in a process that was leading him toward something that most of us just admire from a distance.

You've Got a Friend

I asked my jeet kune do teacher and my father's close friend Ted Wong one time if he could tell me something people might not know about my father, and he said people may not know that he was very caring and generous. He proceeded to tell me a story of how my dad had helped Ted get himself together so that he could find a girlfriend. He said Bruce took him shopping for clothes, cut his hair, helped him buy a weight set, and gave him personalized workout regimens so he could look his best and hopefully get himself a date. Ted went on to meet and marry the love of his life not too long after.

When my father's friend and assistant instructor at his Oakland school, James Lee, was ill and struggling with cancer, my father took over his book project for him, finished it, and got it published so James could have the money from the book to help pay his medical bills.

When my father first met Taky Kimura in Seattle, Taky was very shy and introverted, even though he was sixteen years older than my father. He was struggling with low self-esteem and depression, having been imprisoned in a Japanese internment camp in the United States during World War II. My father struck up a friendship with him and helped him come out of his shell. The two became the best of friends, with Taky becoming his first assistant instructor in his first gung fu school and the best man at my parents' wedding. There are many letters of encouragement and advice that my father wrote throughout his life to Taky. To this day, Taky and his students care for my father's grave in Seattle, and Taky, now ninety-six, still gets tears in his eyes when he thinks about my father's friendship and support.

These are just a few stories of some of his kindnesses, and, of course, there were many people who were kind and supportive of him as well. My mother most of all. I don't bring these stories up because they are extraordinary, but because they were another side of him. One that is expressed in the words "my friend," which he used often to refer not just to his real-life friends but to all his human brothers and sisters, too.

Perhaps as a martial artist it would seem that my father would mostly have a very aggressive and tough presentation (and he could, for sure), but I believe that one of the reasons that my father was so accepting of all humans is precisely because of his experience as a martial artist. He understood that as a basic beginning, we as a human family are more alike than we are different. When he broke from the tradition of styles and pursued fluidity and present, honest expression as his way, it was because he felt that styles separated people. He would often say, "There is no Chinese way of fighting or Japanese way of fighting because unless humans are born with three arms and six legs, then there is no other way of fighting."

Of course, I understand that there are arts that have grown up through particular cultures and masters. He understood this too. And he was into them from an enthusiast point of view. He loved to learn about other masters and arts, especially in his youth. He was fascinated by the ways in which people had created approaches to fighting. But what he means by there's "no Chinese or Japanese way of fighting" is that these cultures and masters (who just happened to be Chinese or Japanese) came up with their way that they felt was most effective or best for the time and circumstance they found themselves in—and so should we. We shouldn't be limited by culture or someone else's ideas. And more important, we shouldn't be threatened by or scornful of other people's ideas. Rather we should accept them alongside our own as their own unique expression.

Now, martial arts may not be your jam. It takes a particular and rather dedicated person to want to investigate combat that deeply for themselves. Most of us who take martial arts begin in one style and stay there because we like it, it's a good workout, or it helps us develop discipline, strength, and confidence, but we aren't going to go that far into an exploration of our own personal and creative style of fighting. At most we may just realize we can execute one technique better or more effectively if we hold our leg slightly this way versus that way. But the point I'm trying to get at is that you should not only use this "Be Water" approach in whatever discipline or work or career path you are on. The point I'm trying to make is that we can apply these ideas and practices to the living of our everyday lives—all of it—work, home, leisure, family, friendship, romantic partnership, business partnership, etc. The thing to connect with is that we are all engaging in a human process every day. All of us.

We are each a creating and expressing entity with our own unique voice and our own unique signature. And we all exist within one family. *One.* The quote at the head of this chapter comes from an interview my father sat for in 1971 where the interviewer, Pierre Berton, a Canadian talk show host, had asked if my father thought of himself as Chinese or North American, and my father replied that he preferred, actually, to think of himself as a human being.

And so, within this context, the last two words of our water journey—*my friend*—suddenly become not just a sweet sign-off, but an extremely important and vital bit of humanity, warmth, encouragement, and unity. My father used the words "my friend" often in his writings. *Go bravely on, my friend. Walk on, my friend. Be water, my friend.*

"My friend" is an arm around your shoulders. It says that he considers you a person with whom he shares a mutual bond. Someone he wants to make a connection with. We've talked a lot about the totality—seeing it all, taking it all in, not judging, not dissecting reality into separate compartments, being in engaged and active relationship, being aligned with nature, going with rather than against an obstacle, changing with change, collaborating rather than competing, creating from the place of nothingness where all options are open and all possibilities available. Well, our fellow humans make up the totality as well. And we want to approach them with the same understanding, care, acceptance, and compassion that we are learning to show ourselves.

This Taoist principle of the integrating whole that cannot be compartmentalized or separated governed my father's way of thinking from very early on. He may not have been consciously aware of it as a child, but as he grew and matured, he began to wake up to and put more emphasis on these ideas and express them. Maybe his personal experiences with race and culture were the impetus for the equal way he approached everyone, but whatever the case, he was not a person who considered people anything other than uniquely interesting by their class, culture, orientation, or race. Those details were the individual embellishments of a shared humanity. More important to him was, how are you showing up as a human? Are you engaged in life? Do you care about your life and self? Are you kind? Are you trying to be a better person? Do your actions and your words match? To him, these were the important factors, not what color your skin was.

My father said, "If every man would help his neighbor, no man would be without help. I'm not one of those guys that can brush people off. Besides, I feel that if I can just take a second to make someone happy, why not do it?"

We hear the words "compassion" and "empathy" and "unconditional love" a lot, and they are good and noble words, but maybe if we start more simply and with something more common that we all have access to, like the word "friend," it could be a path that would eventually lead us to those noble qualities more easily.

To set the intention and take the energy of "friend," "neighbor," or even "acquaintance," if that's all you can muster, and let that energy permeate your interactions could be a major shift in the way you approach the world. Of course, it will have its own challenges as you are faced with having to practice that intention of friend or neighbor with *everyone* and not just the people with whom that is easy to do. But we are here to train ourselves into our fullest potential, so let's train toward acceptance, compassion, and friendship as well.

How we treat everyone is how we treat everyone. Meaning, you may be a good and kind person in the nucleus of your life. But maybe you just can't stand that one neighbor and you're cold to her whenever you see her. Or maybe you despise noisy children and shoot the evil eye at their parents every chance you get. Or maybe you are dismissive of homeless people or talk behind your coworkers' backs or get annoyed with elderly people who move too slowly in front of you or maybe you just don't like people who have cats. The point is, if we are willing to treat some people with disdain, then we are willing to treat the people we care about with disdain as well and we will at some point or another—and we will continue to make it all right to classify people into "the good people" and "the bad people," rather than just "people."

I'm not saying you have to have a kumbaya attitude toward everyone and excuse people's bad behavior. Sometimes you need to take a stand against those who promote fear and hate—but you can still do so with a reverence for life and for humanity. Fighting hate with hate only increases the amount of hate in the world.

Perhaps you can consider that the best way to effect change is by loving the people around you, the people you come into contact with on a daily basis. In your everyday life, give people the benefit of the doubt, treat them with compassion, accept them for who they are, and live and let live while being the light and the model for what it is to be strongly and unapologetically kind. You can and should communicate, love, and try to enroll people in the dream of a harmonious existence, but ultimately, you have no control over anyone but yourself—so how will you behave, how will you respond, and how will you show your respect to humanity?

The True Warrior

In 1971, when my father sat for that interview in Hong Kong with Canadian talk show host Pierre Berton, Pierre asked my father about prejudice in Hollywood. Did it exist? Had my father encountered it? My father said that unfortunately such things did exist and that in fact, because of that very thing, a TV show he was supposed to star in was probably not going to happen for him. But then my father goes on to say something very interesting.

Rather than going on a tirade about how unfair life is or how racist the studio structures in Hollywood are or being incensed about his talent not being recognized, he says instead that he understands. He says, "I don't blame them. It's the same way in Hong Kong. If a foreigner came to become a star, if I were the man with money, I probably would have my own worry of whether or not the acceptance would be there." But he goes on to say that understanding as he may be, this is not going to change his trajectory. For in the same interview he continues, "I have already made up my mind that in the United States something about the Oriental, I mean the *true* Oriental, should be shown." (The word *oriental* was still the term used in the seventies.) And in fact, *not* getting a starring role in a U.S. TV series meant that he went on to make four and a half kick-ass films that traveled the globe and impacted generations of human beings all around the world— something that TV would not have been able to do for him back then. *Not* getting that show put him on a different and more powerful path because he did not become bitter—he remained centered, expressive, and undeterred from his dream. He flowed around that obstacle. And he took action!

He was in on a secret that the studio execs were not. That he, Bruce Lee, was a force to be reckoned with, and that their fear-based thinking was blinding them, and that they didn't understand and value individuals as much as they valued money or fear of criticism or what they believed to be the limited capacity of the American people. And that was *their* shortcoming and not his. So he would go about his business pursuing his dream, expressing his soul, and living his life to the fullest.

Racism and prejudice are traditions passed down from generation to generation. And even if we aren't passing on personal racist beliefs directly, at the very least we do pass on our fears, our bad habits, and our shortcomings while helping to maintain the limiting structures that have been around for generations. The past can't be helped. But what can be helped is how to move beyond these patterns and traditions with some guidance on how we can look at the world if we are open to wanting something better for ourselves and for all.

If we can see and understand and admit our faults and shortcomings, then we have hope for transforming ourselves and thereby our lives and the lives around us. All this knowing oneself, creating this immoveable center that is rooted in our beingness, is what allows us to have compassion for one another.

My father said, "Man, the living creature, the creating individual, is always more important than any established style or system." Stop and take that in for a moment. Do you live that way? Do you make the individual humans around you the most important and valuable parts of life? Or are you more interested in what the cultural institutions tell you that you should think about whole groups of unidentified, face-less humans? What would happen for you in your life if you suddenly became truly interested in the individual lives around you and didn't keep up your barrier of judgment and assumption? What if you got invested in another person's experience or tried to understand what made them who they are? What if you put a figurative or literal arm around their shoulders and thought of them as a friend?

Many people who protest against certain groups of people suddenly change their tune when they discover a personal connection with someone who may be different from them, or when they come to know and love someone who is different from them—gay, black, poor, immigrant, Muslim, whatever it may be. The experience of individual care and attention dissolves the barriers to love. And suddenly love is possible where before only fear existed.

Traditions and institutions can have their benefits, but they do and always will have their limitations, too. An organization or system of belief that has its rules and traditions will always not include someone. Someone will be pushed outside of the boundaries and made "other."

When my father was a teenager at Yip Man's wing chun gung fu school, he was kicked out. Not for bad behavior, but for not being 100 percent Chinese. It was found out that my father's mother was half European, making my father only three-quarters Chinese. The tradition of the time made it such that he could not be considered fully Chinese and thereby he was not allowed to learn Chinese gung fu—and so an uproar ensued. Yip Man did not want to expel my father. In fact, my father was one of his best students, but he could not keep the peace within his school without throwing my father out because the other students threatened to quit if he stayed. This was his livelihood, so Yip Man complied with tradition.

In a work-around, Yip Man continued to train my father in private and have one of his most senior students, Wong Shun Leung, train him as well. But he could not keep him in class. Maybe it was partly this experience that cemented in my father his later policy of taking in anyone to his schools who had a sincere desire to learn, regardless of their race, gender, or background. Maybe it was being a kid growing up in Japanese-occupied Hong Kong during World War II. Maybe it was his commitment to his Taoist philosophical understandings. But the "human first" policy is one I feel we can and really need to all adopt as our barrier to entry for humanity.

My mother always said about my father that he looked straight across at people. Meaning, he looked them in the eye rather than at the embellishments of their outside packaging. His upbringing was such that there were many factors that contributed to this attitude. First of all, he was born in America but raised in Hong Kong. His mother was part European and so he was too. He lived in a primarily Chinese city, but it was governed by the British. He worked in the acting industry as a child, so he spent time around many adults and people with a more creatively open disposition. He experienced racism and prejudice often throughout his life—for being too Chinese in Hollywood and for being too Western in Hong Kong. He often didn't have a tribe to call his own other than his nuclear family, and so he had to make the conscious choice of being exclusive or inclusive. And being inclusive gave him access to many more people, ideas, experiences, friendships, and possibilities. It made his world bigger and more interesting.

> Many people are still bound by tradition; when the elder generations say "no" to something, then these people will strongly disapprove of it as well. If the elders say that something is wrong, then they also will believe that it is wrong. They seldom use their mind to find out the truth and seldom express sincerely their real feeling. The simple truth is that these opinions on such things as racism are traditions, which are nothing more

a "formula" laid down by these elder people's experience. As we progress and time changes, it is necessary to reform this formula. I, Bruce Lee, am a man who never follows the formulas of these fear-mongers. So no matter if your color is black or white, red or blue, I can still make friends with you without any barrier. In saying that "everyone under the sun is a member of a universal family," you may think that I am idealistic. But if anyone still believes in things like racial differences, I think they are too narrow. Perhaps they still do not understand love.

When the Student Is Ready, the Teacher Appears

Remember our principles of yin yang? We talked about how these so called "opposites" are actually related expressions of a totality. And remember the quote about the answer never being apart from the problem, how the answer is the problem? Here's one more shift in perspective for you to consider.

We've talked about making mistakes your friends—cozying up to obstacles until they become opportunities or solutions. We've talked about cultivating mindsets and tools of positivity, enthusiasm, willpower, and more. Now let's talk about making these setbacks your teachers. What does suffering teach? If we really sit with our soul pain, with our constricting ideas and thoughts and ways of being, suffering teaches freedom from suffering. Suffering is such a good teacher because when we are suffering, we want so desperately to stop suffering that we become motivated to try to make it stop. If we want to transmute suffering, if we want to release it, we need to look closely at all the ways in which we cause ourselves suffering, in which we cause others suffering, and learn to move in the other direction back across the scale. We can learn to slide the balance back to a more equitable place. It takes determination and hypervigilance, but the teacher is there and the class is in session if you want to attend. We've seen this through the lens of being the eternal student, and now we have a framework for finding the lesson.

Intolerance can teach tolerance. Judgment can teach acceptance. War can teach peace. Fear can teach love. Shadow can teach light. Open your mind. Rebalance the scale. Look where you've not looked before. When you're on a treasure hunt, you don't just keep looking in the same place over and over if you already know the treasure isn't there. When you can't find your car keys in all the usual places, what do you do? You look in places you can't imagine you would have put them. And sometimes your car keys are in the refrigerator next to the eggs you bought last night. And sometimes they're right where you usually leave them, but for whatever reason you didn't see them the first time. And sometimes you have to tow your car to the dealership and get all new keys because, goddammit, I don't know what happened to those keys!

How much do you want to live a peaceful, alive, joyful life? Enough to tow your car to the dealership? Enough to consider something you never thought you would consider? What's so terrifying about a shift in perspective? It is a change, and I know change can feel risky. But it seems more risky to live an unfulfilling, stuck life that accepts suffering as the norm. Instead why not take on the challenge of choosing to learn from your setbacks, to find the lessons in these teachable moments?

And above all, let's do it in an atmosphere of kindness. Kindness to others who are on their path, but, most important, kindness to ourselves as we find our way. Put that friendly arm around your own shoulders and let go of the shortcomings of the past while you take these lessons forward with you. So many of you have already over-come and lived through some really challenging things. Think of your-selves as superheroes in training. If you're still stuck, that's okay—but beating yourself up over it only makes you feel bad, makes the process unenjoyable, and slows your progress. How would you look upon a friend who was struggling like you are? What can your struggles teach you? How can you show up as both student and teacher? How wide are you willing to open your mind, my friend?

The Key to Immortality

A quote that is often attributed to my dad (because it was placed on the bench that sits across from his grave), but which is in fact not his quote is, "The key to immortality is first living a life worth remem-bering." And so, even though his life was not long in the traditional sense, it has in fact been a very long life—one that we are still sitting here feeling the influence of all these decades later. And though I have spent a good deal of my energy to continue to promote and preserve his legacy, he would have gone on being remembered without me because he did indeed model a life full of inspiration and possibility all on his own.

He was our teacher, our entertainer, our friend, and our family. And his spirit contains the energy of unity and brightness. If I stop to assign an image to the feeling of him for me, it is of golden sunlight shimmering across the rippling ocean waves like a thousand radiant suns. Dazzling you, filling you with wonder, and inviting you forward.

In 2005, a statue was erected of my father in Mostar, Bosnia. It came as much as a surprise to me as it may to you. After the terrible civil war that tore across the region had ended, during which most of the town centers had had their monuments destroyed, the different factions came together to try to decide what monuments to put back. Of course, there was much debate over the various symbols and their meanings, and for a long time they could not reach an agreement.

Until someone suggested that they could erect a statue of Bruce Lee. Yep, that's right. Bruce Lee.

The organizers said of their decision, "One thing we all have in common is Bruce Lee." To them, Bruce Lee represented the fight against ethnic divisions. He was seen as a symbol of someone who bridged cultures and brought people together and made them feel up-lifted.

As for my father, he was never specifically trying for this. In fact, he said of his life and career that he had no idea that what he was practicing would lead to all this. And I'm quite sure he never foresaw a statue in Bosnia. He just lived his life fully and to the highest level of quality and honesty that he could. And we all said, "Wow. Now there is someone real."

As for my father, he did accomplish what he set out to do.

> I don't know what is the meaning of death, but I am not afraid to die. And I go on, non-stop, going forward, even though I, Bruce Lee, may die some day without fulfilling all of my ambitions, I will have no regrets. I did what I wanted to do and what I've done, I've done with sincerity and to the best of my ability. You can't expect much more from life.

Live your life as if this is the life you are living right now—not the life where you will handle stuff one of these days or be happy when this or that happens. This is it. With every moment and every day that passes, this is your life. Remember, you are not striving to be Bruce

Lee. Maybe, in the cultivation of you, you become someone who does what they say they are going to do, someone who is real and fully present, someone who is skilled because they have put time and effort into practicing something important to them, someone who has great energy that uplifts everyone they come into contact with. It doesn't have to come with a name attached—such as greatest martial artist of all time, Nobel prize winner for literature, employee of the month, best mom ever. Remember, names create limitations. Those labels only describe one aspect of your total humanity. But if we have to have a name, then perhaps it can be "human, fully expressed."

Epilogue

I have to leave you now, my friend. You have a long journey ahead of you, and you must travel light. These paragraphs at best have been merely "a finger pointing at the moon." Please do not take the finger to be the moon or fix your intense gaze on the finger and thus miss all the beautiful sight of heaven. After all, the usefulness of the finger is in pointing away from itself to the light that illumines finger and all.

From now on, drop all your burden of preconceived conclusions behind, and "open" yourself to everything and everyone ahead. Remember, my friend, the usefulness of the cup is in its emptiness.

—BRUCE LEE

Acknowledgments

It goes without saying that without my father this book wouldn't exist, but this book doesn't exist without my mother either. My dad wrote the words and created the art, but my mom made it possible (and still does) for all of us to thrive in our pursuits, and together they lived life to the fullest and were a team. Without my mother conscientiously holding on to and exposing me to my father's work all those years while I was growing up, the world would not have gotten such personal insight into Bruce Lee and neither would I. Thank you, Mom, for preserving our family's legacy, for loving me, for teaching me to be kind and caring, and for raising me up to be whoever I wanted to be. I love you.

To Brandon, I miss you every day. Thank you for being such a wonderful big brother and for being there for me in so many ways. Even now, I still feel you with me.

Without my daughter, Wren, I would not have become the more whole and responsible human I am today. Wren, you help me to discover myself. You have been my greatest teacher and my deepest love. You are such a beautiful soul, and I am so grateful for the depth and naturalness of our relationship. It is an honor to be your mother. You're the best daughter ever, and I love you.

To my nuclear Bruce Lee Enterprises Family, Sydnie Wilson, Chris

Husband, Lydy Walker, and Jess Scott, thank you for being so supportive of me. You gave me the time and space to write at home, and you were always so positive and encouraging. You helped me manage the process with such ease—logistics, feedback, digging through the archives, etc. Thank you for being colleagues and friends. And, Sydnie and Chris, thank you for giving me your hearts and not just your heads, for being on this roller-coaster ride with me and holding on tight, and for being my extended family in this life.

A big thank-you to Sharon Lee, without whom there would have been no Bruce Lee podcast. Sharon was the catalyst for the podcast, and the podcast was the catalyst for the book. Had we not had so much fun talking philosophy, I would not have attracted the attention of Albert Lee and Jane von Mehren of the Aevitas Creative Management literary agency. Thank you, Sharon. I am forever grateful for you and your spark!

Albert and Jane, thank you for reaching out to this novice and asking me to write a book—something I'd always secretly wanted to do. How did you know? Your enthusiasm, experience, and guidance has been invaluable. Thank you for helping me find a home for this book, and, Jane, thank you for supporting me throughout the whole process and being such a tremendously caring, warm, and skilled advisor.

Thank you Nicole Tourtelot, who was my aide, my confidante, my second brain, and a skilled technician and writer in her own right. Thank you for walking me through the process from proposal to finished manuscript. Thank you for being my ears and eyes, for listening so intently and consciously, and for helping me to organize and express myself. Your love of the material and your genuine and easygoing personality made this process enjoyable and smooth. I am grateful.

To everyone at Flatiron Books, thank you. There has been and will be so much support from so many of you throughout this process. Please know I am hugely appreciative. Special thanks to Bob Miller, for understanding the project so clearly and being so keen on publishing this book from the outset, and to Sarah Murphy, for your thorough, clear, supportive, and perceptive editing. You are a pleasure to work with and I am so grateful for your affection for the material and your experience and sincere support.

To the painful teachers in my life, thank you. I have grown through our experiences in ways that have been astonishing and profound. I am grateful for the challenges you presented me that made me look more deeply at myself. I have love for you all.

There are too many other beautiful, important people to thank who have helped mold and support me, but I will acknowledge just a few. Joy Margolis, my soul sister; Tony Leroy, my light; Liz Odders-White, my constant friend; Sasa Woodruff, my podcast facilitator, friend, and fellow foodie; Kalyn Cai Bennett, my new friend and giver of wisdom; Dennis Chang and Mike Sullivan, my uplifting, fun, and kick-ass collaborators; and new friends, thank you. Thank you all, for your enthusiasm, for believing in me, guiding me, and supporting me in so many ways. In 2019, I stated that I wanted to create a support system of people who are truly invested in my well-being, and I really feel that I have that with you. Thank you.

And to my father, thank you for being my baba, for loving me so dearly, and for continuing to raise me still.

Be water, my friends.